I0103766

Sunshine and Ice
Volume 7

Persistent Illusions

MARTIN MONEY

Pen Press

© Martin Money 2014

All rights reserved

No part of this publication may be reproduced, stored in a retrieval
system, or transmitted in any form or by any means, without the prior
permission in writing of the publisher, nor be otherwise circulated in
any form of binding or cover other than that in which it is published and
without a similar condition including this condition being imposed on
the subsequent purchaser.

First published in Great Britain

All paper used in the printing of this book has been made from wood
grown in managed, sustainable forests.

ISBN13: 978-1-78003-778-3

Printed and bound in the UK
Author Essentials Ltd
4 The Courtyard
South Street
Falmer
East Sussex BN1 9PQ

A catalogue record of this book is available from
the British Library

Cover design by Jacqueline Abromeit

PERSISTENT ILLUSIONS

(August 2013 – February 2014)

INTRODUCTION – HARDSHIPS

I felt so good on finishing Scratched Crystal. For once, I'd been able to give one of my books a proper, unforced happy ending. I'd achieved my dream, I felt content for the first time in years and things were looking fine in my little corner of existence.

But I did say then that I was refusing to become complacent. I still had a burning desire to continue my searches for truth and my own lost spirituality. I was also driven to intensify my attempts to promote love and justice and become a better person.

And all the time I was fully aware that, although at that particular moment I felt okay, others didn't. We live in a world fractured by madness, sadness and pain. Our televisions will always remind us of that.

Shocking news reports and heart-rending documentaries upset us and make our blood boil. We feel frustrated and largely powerless in the face of such pressing and massive problems and the scale, diversity and severity of the misery they've created.

Some compassionate individuals respond to this sorry state of affairs by rolling up their sleeves, getting stuck in and actually doing something positive to redress the balance, make a difference, and improve things for their fellow citizens.

They deserve our deepest respect, and I say bless them for their endeavours.

Meanwhile, the rest of us just sit on our bums and look around for someone to blame. In my case, this tends to be the politicians from all sides who have created a seriously messed-up system over a very long period of neglect and misrule.

Warped priorities, seriously suspect agendas and vested interests have got in the way of sensible, fair and decent government. And our nation is paying a very high price in the form of all the hassles, hardships and infuriating inconsistencies.

Other people look at the same crises and decide it's the fault of certain sections of society. Those who have come to this country from abroad are favourite targets.

The colour of their skin, the way they dress or their chosen faith make them devils incarnate in some individuals' eyes.

I see this as totally wrong, displaying sickening levels of the bigotry, racism and religious intolerance I detest. And, to state the obvious, these people are only here thanks to the politicians who allowed them to come over and settle in the first place.

For myself, I refuse to blame Muslims, the Polish or any other collective of citizens for the predicament we're in – where poverty is rife, there's a critical shortage of housing, health services are stretched to the limit, the elderly, frail and disabled suffer, children are deprived and abused, and injustice and violence are widespread.

But the politicians would rather play divide and rule – or misrule – ensuring that we turn on each other rather than hold them to account. And I find that despicable…

CHAPTER ONE - SCAPEGOATS

August 5, 2013 – Two things on telly have enraged me in the past 24 hours or so. One was a documentary, the other, a news report.

The documentary, shown for the second time last night, was about council house waiting lists. (I'd missed it first time around).

It told a harrowing tale of thousands of cash-strapped people stuck on these lists for years while vying for the depressingly few low-rent, affordable local authority properties available. It's a horrid, frustrating and deeply distressing national crisis.

Elderly, disabled and frail folk stranded in tower blocks and in dire need of more appropriate accommodation are unwilling locked in fierce competition with single parents whose teenaged sons and daughters are forced to share bedrooms.

Those lucky enough to finally reach the top of the list are then offered a property that may or may not be suitable and could be miles away from their families, friends, doctors' surgeries, schools, shops and other essential facilities.

Regardless of age, state of health or circumstance, they are at that point faced with a stark choice – take what's offered, voluntarily isolating yourself in a daunting, strange new area, or return to the back of the queue after years of waiting.

Whichever way you look at it, this is wrong – scandalously so.

It's a horrific, tinderbox situation carrying the added danger of the desperate turning on each other rather than seeking out and pillorying the politicians whose shameful neglect has caused the problems.

A friend of mine who saw the documentary first time around a few days back seized on the fact that, of six people shown competing for one flat, four appeared to be Muslim women.

My friend was livid, saying English folk who have lived in these areas for generations should get preference.

I can see the point, arguably a very valid one, but to hear the comment phrased the way it was made my blood run cold, for it betrayed all the venom and hatred that desperate situations can generate as the angry seek scapegoats – someone to blame.

Politicians love playing divide and rule and those that think like my friend play right into their hands – targeting the wrong people and letting the real culprits off the hook.

I say vent your rage on those who have created this situation, not other equally deprived and desperate folk caught up in the madness.

It's not the Muslims' fault, any more than it can be pinned on other easy targets such as those of Polish or Romanian extraction.

It's not a racial issue, or a cultural issue – it's a housing crisis, pure and simple, caused by uncaring fools with cocked-up priorities and highly suspect motives.

Turning to the infuriating news item, it was on TV this morning and revealed that up to a million people are on so-called "zero hours contracts" – meaning they're on a payroll but not guaranteed either work or payment.

This is outrageous, and exposes the lie of government assertions that unemployment is falling and more people are in work than ever before.

A zero hours contract means your employer decides if and when you're needed - and you're only paid for those hours. It gives them a vital degree of flexibility when times are hard, and suits some employees just fine – those just topping up other incomes.

But many find themselves in a perilous position, facing a massive hurdle. For they rely heavily on these jobs to supply vital funds, and are deemed to be in regular work - therefore denied any state benefits during lean times when they have no income.

Job security has been a thing of the past for decades now, but it's shocking and very worrying to learn just how serious the problem is.

To state the obvious, people still have to pay for food, accommodation and other essentials whether they're in paid work or not. No wonder they're getting fractious, stressed and angry, desperately seeking someone to vent their rage upon.

And, once again, they'd rather hit out at other ordinary citizens than go after the politicians - Labour, Tory and now Lib-Dem - who have jointly created this dreadful and totally unacceptable set of circumstances over many years.

August 6 - I saw a TV advert last night that summed up a disturbing trend – the deliberate and accelerating merging of the lines between fact and fiction.

The commercial was for Marmite – which I don't like anyway, but that's by the by. Even if I had liked the product, I would still have been deeply offended by the tone and content of this cynical attempt to sell it.

The advert was quite bizarrely made in the style of one of those terminally tedious, irritatingly smug, fly-on-the-wall documentaries alleging flagrant abuses, made by people who think they're perfect and everyone else is badly flawed.

It was the latest in a string of such commercials impersonating real life situations – some even deliberately sandwiched in the breaks between actual news bulletins.

No wonder people get mixed up over what's real and what isn't. I'm convinced this works in favour of certain sinister individuals in very influential positions who specialise in spreading confusion in order to retain control.

Like spin doctors and stage magicians, they create a mesmerising muddle of mixed messages and persistent illusions that keep us all dazzled, spellbound and powerless.

These annoying, mind-numbing adverts help further muddy the waters, and I find the whole toxic mess highly undesirable and quite alarming.

And speaking of persistent illusions, let's not forget that the so-called reality we're programmed to accept from cradle to grave is the biggest, most persistent illusion of them all.

****

August 7 – To lighten the mood somewhat, I'm pleased as punch to report that I'm properly reunited with my very dear friend Steve Yarwood.

It's happened thanks to our mutual buddy Jem Hannen – for it was he who invited both of us to join him for a couple of beers at Seabourne's Bar (The Bell) a fortnight ago.

Cheers Jem, mate - you're an absolute star!

I hadn't seen Steve for some nine months – he'd basically cut himself off from pretty much everyone, me included, needing time on his own to grapple with his health issues and other worries that had seriously messed with his head.

He was almost ready to re-emerge when I gave his long-time partner Jill a copy of Sunshine and Ice Volume One to pass on to him.

He'd read it all in one go within hours of receiving it - and sent me a text in the early hours of the following day to congratulate me in his own unique, hilarious, back-handed way.

That was the first contact I'd had from Steve for three quarters of a year, during which he'd lived like a hermit, kept a low profile and taken himself off Facebook.

He'd just come back on to it when Jem decided it was high time the three of us met up again. Steve's now re-friended me and other former Facebook pals (Jem's not on it).

And the two of us have seen each other twice since that pub reunion. He's been round mine for tinnies, mad times and some right hilarious conversations.

God, I have so missed those crazy, funny sessions! I think I can confidently say that the Tuesday Night Club is about to be re-launched big style – but on Wednesdays!

To quote Steve himself: "All aboard the Skylark!"

It's just bloody marvellous to be back in regular contact with one of the best and closest male friends I've ever had.

And it was so wonderfully appropriate that it happened thanks to our very good pal Jem. As Steve philosophically observed: "It was meant to be."

Sadly, Steve and Jill have finally called it a day after 14 years together. But they've parted without acrimony or bitterness and remain very good friends, which is great.

I still see Jill quite regularly – she works at the launderette I use. She's a sweetheart, a real hippie chick. I like her a lot and wish her all the best

Incidentally, yesterday was my old mate big Sam's birthday and today is Tina Wilkins.' I wish them the very warmest of greetings, too.

On a sadder note, my friend Jaymi Darragh is grieving at the moment, having said a final farewell to her mum at

Bournemouth Crematorium yesterday. I dearly hope Jaymi and her family can support each other through these dark times.

August 18 – My sister Carol and her husband David have been married 40 years today. And my friends Tina and Jeff McNally are celebrating their 12th wedding anniversary. Many congratulations to both couples!

Congrats also to Big Sam (Kevin Sansom), who I've just learned married his long-time girlfriend Sue the other day.

August 21 – I'm thinking of my good friend Sam Excell, who's mourning the passing of her beloved dad, Jim, seven years ago today. I've lit a candle for him.

I remember Jim from the Home Guard social club, many moons ago. To be honest, I didn't know him all that well, but everyone knew his brother Cess, the bar manager.

Today is also Andy Frend's birthday. Have a good one, mate!

August 22 – More good news! Alison Quilter, a new friend of mine and Phil's step-sister, gave birth to a little girl, Roxanna, yesterday morning. Mum and baby are doing fine and proud dad Terry Russ is overjoyed.

You may recall my journal entry of a month ago when I said Ali and Terry had just moved from Ferndown to Southbourne and I'd spent a pleasant morning after taking up Ali's invitation to pop round for coffee and a chat.

Births and deaths, weddings and anniversaries, smiles and sadness, ups and downs – they're all part of life's roller-coaster.

August 24 – Yesterday evening was a belter – I saw Hawkwind at Boscombe's O2 Academy. And they were brilliant – much better than the last time I saw them a few years ago at the Bournemouth International Centre.

On that occasion, the band was just founder-member Dave Brock and two other lesser-known guys, supported by other musicians and dancers. They were good, but not a patch on the line-up when I saw them on the Levitation tour in 1980.

I've seen this group on four occasions now, more than any other famous rock act. Okay, the first time, back in 1978, they were calling themselves Hawklords but the personnel included both Bob Calvert and Dave Brock (though not Nik Turner) and to many fans they were still Hawkwind in all but name.

Last night was excellent, right back up to the Levitation and Hawklords standard. I went with Carl but we met other friends there, including Jem, his girlfriend Debs, Jem's brother Tony, Andy Frend, Chris and Louise and a guy I've known for ages nicknamed Gary the Sheep because he's Welsh (he's a jovial soul and doesn't mind).

Chris and Lou are both really nice people and I attended their wedding a few years ago.

Needless to say, yesterday evening was a triumph, in terms of both great music and fine company.

August 27 – Yippee! Sunshine and Ice Volume Two is out – I received my paperback copies this morning. It comprises the books Descent into Darkness and Déjà vu, covering the period from just after the assault on me in December 2001 to the end of 2005.

I'm going to be giving out free copies to some of my mates – especially the ones who have been nice about volume one.

Those mates will include Sam and Carl, who staged an impromptu barbeque in the sun yesterday afternoon. They supplied the grill and venue and our mutual friend Tina took along the food.

Tina's bloke Lou provided booze and so did I. Sam's little boys Rudy and Bailey and her teenaged daughter Becca were also there. Very pleasant it was, too.

August 31 – I went to Sam and Carl's yesterday and took along signed copies of volume two for them and other friends who visit them. I also popped two personalised copies in to Kerry's for her and Theresa.

 I've posted others and, a couple of days ago, I dropped off a few at Jem's - again, for him and other mates he sees more often than I do.

I gave Steve Yarwood two signed copies – one for him, the other for Jill – and I delivered one to Darren Williams and another to Chris (as in Chris and Louise).

I said to Carl yesterday that, on reading my series of haphazard ramblings, friends who always thought I was nuts will now know for certain that I am!

Yesterday was Jem's 49th birthday. Happy birthday sausage!

Turning to more serious matters, 1,400 people are said to have died in a poison gas attack in Syria, blamed on government forces.

It's the latest shocking turn of events in that country's bitter and bloody civil war.

But the gas allegation takes the crisis to an alarming new level as critics in the West start sabre-rattling, banging on about such chemical weapons use breaching international law.

America is leading the charge, threatening military intervention to halt what it says is the unacceptable slaughter of innocent civilians by savage overlords acting illegally.

Our own Prime Minister, David Cameron, asked the Commons two days ago to join the USA in launching a limited but effective missile attack.

The motion was narrowly defeated – thank goodness – but the volatile Syrian situation is a cause for global concern.

I hear sinister echoes of the Iraq debacle with talk of weapons inspectors being shot at while uncovering evidence of unlawful use of banned devices intended to cause mass destruction.

And I fear that further allegations will follow as more spin and pressure are brought to bear to persuade our own Parliament and populace to back America's intervention plan. We could then become embroiled in yet another very costly military adventure on foreign soil.

This would once again rub salt in the wounds of those hit by job and benefits cuts while putting us firmly in the sights of radical extremists fighting Western intervention in the Middle East. Thanks a bunch guys!

Isn't it strange how governments driven by a brutal zeal to fiscally shaft their own citizens while pleading poverty can always find cash to fight wars?

September 1 – Sir David Frost has passed on, felled by a heart attack at the age of 74. He was a broadcasting legend and will be greatly missed.

His most famous moment probably came when his fierce interrogation of disgraced US president Richard Nixon broke the man's resistance and got him to admit he'd lied and let his country down. It was a riveting piece of TV history.

Frost interviewed several prime ministers among a host of world-famous people, including massive stars in many fields - and was noted for his skills of putting people at their ease and catching them off guard, making for some top-notch telly.

But for me his finest legacy remains his massive contribution to British comedy – Pete and Dud, the Pythons, the Goodies, Marty Feldman and the Two Ronnies were among the critically-acclaimed stars he gave vital breaks to on his trailblazing shows.

September 3 – It's turning into a very bad week for TV legends – and it's only Tuesday! Hot on the heels of David Frost's demise at the weekend, we now learn the shock news that David Jacobs has also passed on, aged 87.

Like Frost, he also started off on radio before switching to TV with ease, similarly carving himself an indelible name as a giant of broadcasting.

Jacobs' career spanned seven decades and he fulfilled a wide range of TV presenter roles. One of his most famous was as

"Mr Juke Box Jury" the original and by far the best presenter of the much-watched panel show on which celebrities were asked whether they thought freshly-released pop records would be a "hit" or a "miss."

I remember one programme in particular where the four panellists were the Beatles. No idea why!

But Jacobs, like Frost, had an amazing ability to put people at their ease. And, by all accounts, he was a really nice guy too – a well-spoken, well-mannered gentleman, with a terrific sense of humour.

On other news, the Syrian civil war rages on with increased pressure for us to join in. Please no – but it's looking more and more inevitable.

September 4 – Meanwhile, government ministers continue with their ridiculous, insensitive and positively insulting claims that our once proud nation is on the road to recovery. What total bollocks!

Quite recently, I posed the question – where, oh where are the voices of protest and forceful yet peaceful demonstrations against devastating coalition policies?

One possible answer is that they've been silenced and stifled by the serious erosion of civil liberties in these paranoid post-911 times.

But a thought occurred to me last night while watching a TV programme about computer hacking. Maybe cyber-rebellion is the new form of disruption – taking on the corrupt establishment via the internet.

They say information is more valuable than diamonds or platinum these days. Its misuse and manipulation can certainly have serious consequences. Welcome to the 21st century!

September 14 – Well, I'm back at my computer and it's time to resume my journal after a week away.

I went with Sam, Carl, Sam's grown-up kids Alex and Becca and her and Carl's two little boys Rudy and Bailey, plus Sam's cousin Jac, to spend four days in a caravan at Haven's Sea View holiday park just outside Weymouth.

Alex, who's 18, had to return home Wednesday afternoon to work that evening – he's a trainee chef at a Bournemouth restaurant. And Alex and Becca's dad, Russell, came to stay Thursday night with his gorgeous and affectionate Staffie bitch Lola.

It was a very enjoyable break from my normal routine in good company with a welcome change of scenery.

One particular highlight was a visit to Weymouth's Sea Life Centre, with its indoor tanks and outdoor pools holding a wealth of exotic marine life including sharks, giant turtles, penguins, piranhas, stingrays, anemones and massive crabs and eels.

But it's still good to be back home again in familiar surroundings – my modest little flat with my own bed, kitchen, bathroom, armchair, telly, music centre and so on.

And I'm off to King's Park up the road from me later today (a Saturday) for the annual Boscombe Community Fair - a sort of mini-festival with live music, stalls, kids' entertainment, a bar, food vans and suchlike.

It's the 18th birthday year of the event, which raises money for local community projects. I love it - it's a bit of gathering of the clans and I usually bump into friends I haven't seen for ages.

September 15 – Ah yes – Boscombe Community Fair. Great music, my kind of people! And if you don't know what that means, then you clearly haven't been paying attention!

September 16 – I returned to the fair yesterday afternoon and had another mighty fine time listening to some fab sounds in the company of good mates.

On Saturday, the rain had kept off and it turned out to be a nice day. This time, we sheltered in a tent, ignoring the heavy showers outside. Hardcore or what? Ha ha!

I spent a fair bit of time both days with Tina and Jeff McNally. On Saturday, I also saw Tony Hannen (Jem's brother) and Maria Harris. And yesterday I bumped into Jaymi Darragh, who I hadn't seen for a while.

The consistently excellent but diverse line-up of groups included Voodoo Vegas, The Kleeks, Just Us and Her, the Sporadics and Fearne. (I missed the headline acts as I arrived and left the event early both days).

To bring us bang up to date, I must wish my good mate Roz Tidiman a very happy birthday. I sent her a Facebook message this morning and hope she's okay, as I haven't seen her to talk to for over a year.

There was an item on today's TV news about government plans to introduce 10-year maximum prison sentences for benefit cheats.

Yes, it's a serious matter and some persistent offenders need to be punished, but come on – that's demented! Are these deluded head cases actually telling us that defrauding the system is as bad as raping someone, beating them to a pulp, robbing them at knifepoint or waving a shotgun in their face?

Shows how ruddy screwed up their priorities are. Oh yes, it's bad to violently abuse or scare the shit out of your fellow citizen but no worse than taking money from an amorphous collective where no-one is bodily harmed. Brilliant!

Oh, and what about greedy MPs who fiddle their expenses – are they going to be as severely dealt with? – Because fraud is fraud, no matter how privileged your position.

The news channel also told us that comedian Billy Connolly has had an operation for prostate cancer and is also suffering from the first stages of Parkinson's disease. I'm sure we all wish this comedy legend the very best.

September 19 – It seems people all over the country are facing eviction and homelessness thanks to a new tax on glorified storage spaces.

Their housing benefit has been cut, forcing them into arrears, because under new government rules the tiniest of box rooms are being classed as extra bedrooms.

This move is supposedly to ensure that no-one is living in – and claiming benefit for – a home bigger than they need. But smaller places aren't that easy to come by, so many are stuck, unable to move even if they wanted to.

The highly controversial, so-called "bedroom tax" is yet another glaring example of this heartless coalition's war on its own people – and especially the less well-off.

Citizens can no longer afford to pay their rent on time, so they fall into debt. Landlords have the choice of letting them do so – avoiding the hassles of redecorating and finding new tenants – or chucking them out on the streets.

Result? - More unfairness, more worry, more misery and bitterness and more divide and rule. In other words, a further fractured and fragmented nation. It's sickening!

September 19, five hours later – What a lovely surprise! Phil phoned this morning to ask if I was in today. He was taking time off work and Emily and he were on the rounds visiting family members.

About half an hour later, they arrived at mine with baby Chloe and little Harvey – making his first-ever visit to my home (Lucas was with his mum). We spent a fab couple of hours together, chatting, catching up and posing for photos. Brilliant!

Shifting Sand

Martin Money, September 19-21, 2013.

Fact and fiction, hurt and friction, silk and razor's edge
Fake elections, chipped reflections, muck to shift and dredge
Crazy leaders – vicious bleeders! – Shrill division bell
Message mixers, shady fixers dragging us to Hell.

Lost in mazes, spells and phases, nothing seems to last
Scared and anxious, tense and fractious – yearning for the
past
Hocus pocus, losing focus, sucked into the mire
Politics and dirty tricks cast dreams into the fire.

Those things I thought were carved in stone
Were scrawled in shifting sand
As gospels changed and rules were bent
By fortune's fickle hand.

Anger's growing, claws start showing, crossroads up ahead
Time to change course, feel that love force kill the fear and
dread
Fresh perspective, lose invective, regain inner peace
Spread the joy man, form a new plan, start with days like
these.

September 23 – It's 2.30pm and I've had a very good day so far. This morning I sauntered through Fisherman's Walk to the cliff top to sit for half an hour enjoying the fresh air and the superb views over Bournemouth Bay.

It was so peaceful and therapeutic and I resolved to do this more often now the busy summer season's finished.

While there, I phoned Steve Yarwood, found out he was at home and then took a five minute walk to his flat, which is on the way back to mine. I stayed there for a couple of hours, having coffee and a chat with my great mate. Result!

September 24 – A British-born woman is allegedly among Muslim terrorists killing more than 60 people in an armed siege at a Kenyan shopping mall. Six Britons are among the dead and over 50 individuals are still missing.

Meanwhile, American president Barack Obama continues to press the United Nations to take a tough stance and consider swift, effective military intervention in Syria, where an oppressive regime is said to be using internationally-banned chemical weapons against its own people.

Some say this is just the cover story as the West carries out its brutal campaign to gain and retain control of the Middle East, stealing land and resources.

And I'm starting to wonder - just what is it with this guy Obama?

When he came to power, we celebrated as the first black man ever took charge of our superpower ally nation. And he was a Democrat. The future looked brighter for the US in particular and the west in general.

But since then, he's appeared to be just as ruthless and shifty as his white predecessors, both Republican and, surprisingly, Democrat (Carter and Clinton).

I've even read some stunning allegations that his stance and comments echo those of Adolf Hitler on his rise to power in Germany – before all that dictator's talk of democracy and hope gave way to savage Nazi rhetoric and murderous policies.

I wouldn't go that far, but I do now seriously doubt the integrity and motives of the US leader, especially in light of his sabre-rattling over foreign affairs.

And it might be worth remembering that the Germans trusted Hitler until it was too late and the full horror of his warped vision was brought to bear on a shocked Europe.

September 26 – More than 350 people have perished and thousands of homes been flattened by an earthquake in Pakistan. Kinda puts our problems into perspective, don't you think?

Concerns about my health aside, one of my biggest issues in recent years has been my disgraceful treatment at the hands of uncaring and positively spiteful benefits offices, detailed at some length in my journal as the whole sorry saga unfolded.

Granted, this pales into insignificance compared to the death and destruction being inflicted on other parts of the world – and even our own country. But my anxiety and anger were completely justified – I did have very good grounds for complaint.

Stuck on benefits, I would have been content continuing to draw the dole when I went into hospital first time around but was heavy-handedly told I couldn't and I would therefore need to claim sickness benefit instead.

Although faced with this extra hassle at a time I was pretty damned worried about my state of health, I complied and started receiving ESA.

One big advantage of this was that I was getting about £30 extra a week while laid up, unable to spend it.

This was a nice side-effect of my crisis, but I was only doing as I was told to protect crucial benefit payments and I've never been able to fathom out the weird logic behind it!

Anyway, a year passed as I grappled with my second, far more horrendous hospital experience and its devastating aftermath - physically, mentally and emotionally.

Patently unfit for work, I carried on getting the sickness benefit I'd only asked for in the first place because I had no choice. Then, without warning, it was axed with no offer of alternative funding – even though I still had a valid doctor's certificate!

Not only that, I was threatened with my housing benefit being withdrawn as well, leaving me financially high and dry while already in considerable mental turmoil.

My appeal against this cruel injustice was rejected and I was told – again, very heavy-handedly - to claim jobseeker's allowance – even though I was still far from fit for any kind of paid work.

I ask you, is this fair? No wonder I've ended up bitterly pissed off with the whole crazy, illogical and inconsistent benefits system!

But I still feel for those affected by the Pakistan earthquake and other tragic events at home and abroad. Like I said, it reminds you there are always people a lot worse off than you are. And it's worth bearing that in mind – constantly!

September 29 – As if to hammer home that last point, hot on the heels of the earthquake comes another slice of bad news for the people of Pakistan – this time involving over 30 deaths in a bomb blast. Our hearts go out to their families.

For myself, I've had a good weekend. Friday evening I went to Seabourne's (The Bell) where I saw my mate John Gaynor and gave him a copy of Sunshine and Ice Volume Two.

I also saw my pals Rebecca Browning, John Palmer, Ben Avill, Vicky Brown, Matt Brandt, Ollie Okoye, Kelly Adams and my close neighbour and friend Billy Clarkson.

It was a better session than most due to the number of familiar faces turning up at the same time – a rare occurrence in that pub these days!

And yesterday, Saturday, I spent a few hours at Sam's with her, Carl, Rudy, Bailey, Becca and Rich Jeffery. Sweet!

Today is my very dear friend Lorna Lane's birthday. I sent her a message by Facebook this morning.

Readers of my earlier books might remember that Lorna and Sue Bolton are former work colleagues of mine from Mace, the charity telemarketing firm then situated above the One

Stop convenience store a couple of minutes' walk from my home.

They're also first-class drinking buddies and we've had some right good laughs together.

September 29, evening – I've just watched Close Encounters of the Third Kind for the umpteenth time on TV. It's a brilliant film – Spielberg at his very best – with an excellent performance by Richard Dreyfuss as the bewildered hero.

Apart from being a cracking story stylishly presented, this movie poses two big questions – do aliens exist, and could they at some point make contact with us?

Opinions are bound to vary, and some will claim they already have. Roswell, Area 51 and a host of other related subjects come into focus as conspiracy theorists go into overdrive.

As I've said more than once, I retain an open mind to all possibilities and feel that, while some of these theories might contain at least a germ of truth, others will be complete hogwash.

Writing them all off as fantasy would be as reckless as believing the whole lot without hesitation.

At which point, the word "gullible" springs to mind. Some would no doubt consider me to be gullible in giving alternative explanations and apparently outlandish scenarios the time of day.

But I just think I'm being balanced and sensible. To me, "gullible" is the poor sap who believes the toxic bull crap peddled by some Fleet Street papers, or those who accept without question what someone else tells them about history or religion without applying any analytical thoughts of their own.

Adopting another person's slant on the truth because you can't be bothered to formulate your own is just plain lazy, in my view.

Of course, whether gullible, lazy or analytical, we all find that huge chunks of our own worldview are the same or very similar to our peers' anyway – some more, some less – but no two lives are identical so surely our paradigms shouldn't be either?

Truth is truth. It can be found in diverse places and if you're tuned in to your deepest instincts – you inner self – you will know in your heart of hearts if something sounds or feels right or not.

Tragically, far, far too many people – most of us, actually – aren't tuned in anything like as often as we should be.

Some aren't at all, their existences so cluttered with trivialities they've lost any sight of a spiritual aspect.

And if that's me being gullible, I will proudly accept the description. Wouldn't have it any other way!

September 30 – In fact, I'd much rather be branded gullible than crazy and spiteful like Chancellor of the Exchequer George Osborne.

Obnoxious Osborne was on the TV news today unveiling his iron fist plans for the long-term unemployed.

Those who have been on a work programme for two years – therefore jobless for three – will be instructed to either do community work or turn up at the jobcentre every single day in order to continue receiving benefits.

Frigging hell – severe or what! Is this guy really that alarmingly right-wing, or just plain bonkers? Either way, he's dangerous because of his power.

Firstly, these so-called work programmes are bloody useless in providing new employment opportunities. In fact, they're an expensive joke.

Secondly, his bold but ridiculous claim that jobs are being created in the economy flies in the face of all the facts.

Thirdly, he says he wants to get rid of the "something for nothing" culture. Again, this shows just how totally out of touch he is.

People receiving the miserly jobseeker's allowance aren't living in the lap of luxury as he suggests – they're struggling to make ends meet.

Most will not be within walking distance of a jobcentre or their allotted community project – so they'll have to find bus fares every day from their meagre benefits.

If they drive cars, it will mean more petrol money. But if they do, it begs the obvious question how on Earth can they afford to? – I certainly couldn't when I was on welfare.

Plus, of course, all the time and energy these people will be wasting attending job-starved jobcentres or performing community duties will take them away from their vital task of hunting for any of the increasingly scarce real paid work vacancies.

And fourthly, even if employers have positions they want to fill – a rare occurrence these days – they certainly won't be willing to take on anyone who's been apparently inactive for that length of time. Would you?

Also, I found to my horror that when my JSA or ESA payments were threatened, so was my Housing Benefit – leaving me facing the grim prospect of being both penniless and homeless.

Have the rules changed since then? – I don't know – but even without this added worry, benefit claimants are being screwed and screwed again by this vicious administration just because they're easy targets. And that's despicable!

What really stinks is the undisguised glee with which Osborne and Cameron deliver their devastating body blows to their fellow citizens. How sadistic can you get?

Don't get me wrong – I'm all for unemployed people doing tasks that will get them back into working mode while giving them useful skills they could use if and when they do find paid employment.

But this should be purely voluntary - if they're fit and healthy enough and actually want to do it. Forcing folk to do anything is seriously counter-productive because it just generates resentment where there should be enthusiasm and inspiration.

And all this raises the question – how much does a Trident missile cost? Or a new high-speed rail link for that matter? Because if saving money is these coalition cut-throats' primary aim, as they claim, surely expensive hardware should be sacrificed first – not flesh and blood people in the country they're supposed to be running.

But then, if you believe the government's cobblers about the need to cut costs, you really are being gullible! It's all about bitter division and total control.

And our callous overlords are ably assisted by our good friends in the media. Highlighting Osborne's latest dreadful plan this morning, the BBC TV news interviewed a woman from Gingerbread, the single parents' charity.

She was firmly opposing the move, fearing it would unfairly hit single parents stuck on jobseeker's allowance.

The woman was being interviewed by a bloke – and the ignorant clot then said something really stupid about the need for such people to seek and find work.

This made me cringe. It made me realise that yes, there actually still are some people in this world who can't see that being a parent is the hardest and most important job of all. A staggering fact, I know, but tragically true.

I've just had a thought. I've just referred to obnoxious Osborne. We also have creepy-crawly, compliant Clegg and his despicable capitulation to hard line Tory policies. Now I need another word starting with "C" to describe Cameron. Hmm.

Speaking of devious David, our wonderfully enlightened, kind and compassionate Prime Minister was on TV yesterday, being interviewed about various policies including where he stood on immigration and terrorism.

He said we should be able to ensure that people posing a serious threat to our nation are chucked out of the country.

Okay, Dave – I'll help you pack!

Golden Dawn

Martin Money, September 29-30 2013.

With the face of an angel and the body of a porno star
She takes coke with her coffee and her lunch at a salad bar
Yes, her mad contradictions are the signs of a warped, broken
mind
If you scratch at the surface, it's amazing what terrors you'll
find.

He's the trailblazing zealot of a bright new world order sharp
and clear
But it's cold and metallic and the whole crazy vision's based
on fear
And we're shackled to steel on their skull-covered pirate ships
We're their slaves, pure and simple, robbed of thought by our
own micro-chips.

Welcome to the golden dawn where love's destroyed and hate
reborn
Where truth is managed, facts are changed and poison seeps
from brains deranged.

****

CHAPTER TWO - MORALS

October 2 – On the face of it, morality is a pretty clear-cut, black and white issue. Each of us can state with some certainty what we feel is right or wrong.

Whether guided by religious teachings or an inbuilt sense of decency and humanity, we can all agree that murder, brutal exploitation, robbery and deception are all definite no-nos – especially if they involve children.

But then context and circumstance get in the way to mess things up.

For instance, killing is generally regarded as wrong. But swatting an insect to stop it biting you or slaughtering animals to be used as food are both widely accepted.

Most parents asked if they would die for their offspring would respond with an immediate, loud and emphatic "yes." It's a no-brainer, surely, the way it should be, and anyone hesitating would be viewed as cowardly, weird or just plain evil.

But ask them if they would kill to protect their families. This is a much tougher question to answer, because we all know that inflicting death or injury is beyond the pale. No riders, no excuses – wrong, full stop.

But understandable or even justified in certain situations? Stern morality says "no way" but basic instinct, sheer humanity and common decency often scream "yes."

The world is full of contradictions and vociferous people brashly telling us what they'd do if this or that crisis hit them or their families.

But none of us knows for sure what exactly our response would be in the heat of the moment, faced with a snap decision. This is the stark reality of human weakness.

Those shocking themselves and others by choosing to save their own skins would have to live with that decision for the rest of their lives. And rightly so.

And here's a real moral mind bender. If someone involved in dodgy or diabolical deeds then gives some of the funds they've amassed to worthy causes, is that money forever tainted and the gesture therefore tarnished, corrupted and invalidated?

Or could it be argued that money is neutral but its energy can switch from positive to negative and back again depending on how it's used? I can appreciate and respect the former view but personally lean towards the latter.

I believe that, no matter how the cash was raised, its employment for good, altruistic purposes somehow cleanses and purifies it, cancelling out any bad stuff involved in its accumulation. But this can also work in reverse.

These are just two examples of how morality is a complex conundrum, nowhere near as sharply defined as we would like it to be.

Right, that's quite enough of the heavy shit for now. I've just returned from a great day out in Poole with my very good buddy Steve Yarwood.

As I put on Facebook a few minutes ago, it was a very pleasant excursion for two ageing gits growing old disgracefully and not really giving a toss. Soapbox Steve and Moaner Martin. Ha ha!

While in Poole, I picked up a real bargain in the shape of some excellent films on DVD – The Lord of the Rings trilogy, the first three Terminator movies and Kill Bill Volumes One and Two…and all for £14.50p!

October 3 – I watched Kill Bill Two last night. Like all Quentin Tarantino's work, it's brilliantly and stylishly constructed and presented. Uma Thurman is the main star but David Carradine plays the Bill of the title.

Seeing him again sent my mind drifting back to the 1970s when I first encountered him in the lead role of the classic American television series Kung Fu.

It was set in the Wild West but Carradine played a Shaolin monk and martial arts expert, so the whole enterprise was drenched in eastern spirituality.

It was groundbreaking, highly original and I loved it – even though doing so unnerved me a fair old bit at the time.

Why? – Because I was then still very much rooted in the Christian Methodist worldview I was brought up to respect and adhere to. Sure, I had already started shaking loose, but I remained confused and uncertain where I was heading.

My adopted paradigm was so deeply ingrained that it unsettled me to find such profound stuff in a TV show expounding a strange, unfamiliar but undeniably intriguing way of seeing things that sounded so right – like eternal wisdom.

Since then, of course, my evolving spiritual mindset has embraced glittering gems of wisdom from all sorts of diverse places, both within the boundaries of organised religion and outside it.

Truth is truth no matter where you find it and no faith has a monopoly on enlightenment. Mystics come in all shapes, sizes and colours, from a wide range of backgrounds. And the sooner the world realises that, the better.

October 6 – I was dancing with tygers yesterday evening. Or rather, I was swaying on the spot, nodding my head, tapping my foot and drumming my hand on my leg to the excellent sounds of the Tygers of Pan Tang heavy rock group.

I saw them at Mr Kyps, a small live music venue in Parkstone, Poole. My mate Carl took me along in his car, and we both enjoyed some mighty fine fast and loud rock and roll.

Its some 30 years since I last saw the Tygers, at Bournemouth Town Hall. They were impressive then, and still were last night.

I seem to be making a habit of leaving it three decades to see great hard rock bands a second time. In February, it was UFO in Boscombe.

Just goes to prove that ageing rockers stubbornly refuse to fade into the background with anything resembling grace or dignity. They keep on rolling while drawing their pensions. Cool!

October 8 – "There's a dinosaur on your stairs!" is not something you expect to hear every day.

But, to explain, I was at the home of friends for their boy's third birthday. And I was reporting accurately on what I was seeing - not hallucinating at all!

My apparently bizarre comment was made to my mate Sam as I nipped up to the loo at hers and saw the two-foot plastic dinosaur toy – I guess one of her son Rudy's presents – on the staircase leading to the first floor.

It was a jolly good party, and Rudy seemed to enjoy it. There was the usual birthday cake, nibbles and decorations. And quite a few presents for him to open.

Also in attendance were Sam's man Carl, their other son Bailey – Rudy's little brother - Sam's two adult kids Alex and Becca, their dad Russell, and mutual friends Tina Mcauley and Rich Jeffrey.

Rich brought along his grown-up daughter Stacey and several other younger family members. Becca's mate Shannon was there with her baby girl, and a schoolgirl called Storm, Kelly Adams' daughter, was as good as gold playing with the younger ones and helping keep them entertained.

That was yesterday afternoon. And today, it's Alex's 19th birthday, so I'll be meeting him at Seabourne's pub later to buy him a pint before he heads into town for a late one with his mates.

Interestingly, Sam's two other kids' birthdays are also very close together - Bailey's is April 29 and Becca's, May 1.

October 11 – I've notched up a notable first – I've joined a political party. Yep, I've decided to nail my colours to the Green mast.

Why? – Because on reading their manifesto and books explaining their policies and philosophies, and watching TV coverage of their recent national conference, I feel their vibrant, radical worldview dovetails very nicely with my own on so many burning issues facing our societies and our planet.

For years, I voted Liberal, then Liberal Democrat. But it never occurred to me to join that party. Granted, of the three main ones, it reflected my views more closely than either Labour or the Conservatives.

But I never truly bought into that vision with the same enthusiasm I now have for the Green agenda.

Plus, of course, I've long had an inbuilt distrust of politicians. And, initially, I was a journalist so could not be seen to be showing any bias. But come polling time I consistently chose them.

Then Clegg and his cohorts came along and severed that link forever.

Like all their supporters, I was over the moon when the last general election threw up the hung-Parliament scenario and they got into Downing Street by default – in truth, the only way they were ever going to do so.

They held the balance of power and had the chance to exert a real influence in halting unfair, vicious, hard line right wing policies in their tracks.

I reported my delight in my life journal at the time. I really thought this new set-up could work, where the previous Labour administration had started to resemble shambling wannabe Tories who'd run out of ideas and were leading the nation to ruin.

But I was shocked, angered and bitterly disappointed by the disgraceful betrayal of pure Liberal ideals and attitudes that followed. I vowed never to vote for them again.

I could not believe how Clegg - a man I'd had so much respect for before that election, and voted for without hesitation as he seemed to be making all the right noises - could so easily climb into bed with the Conservatives.

He and his shady pals just rolled over and allowed Cameron's cut-throats to inflict their brutal and unfair Tory agenda without a hint of protest. Disgraceful!

This merely strengthened my aversion to politics in general and politicians in particular, seeing them as devious players more interested in power than principles.

So it comes as quite a surprise to me - let alone anyone else - that I've now decided to take the plunge and identify myself so closely with the Greens.

Let's face it; I'm hardly an eco-warrior. I eat meat, wear leather, and don't buy that many so-called green products.

But I do hate cruelty to animals. I'm all for free-range farming and advocate that any slaughter that provides us with food is done with the minimum of suffering.

I totally oppose testing cosmetics on creatures – except willing Homo sapiens - but grudgingly accept their limited use in experiments if it can be proven beyond doubt that human lives might be saved or improved by any findings.

I support recycling but think local councils should do it– not pass the buck to us. And I'm furious over plans for shops to charge us for flimsy plastic bags that fall to bits before we've got them home, preventing us re-using them (recycling) anyway.

Methinks this move – like recycling rules, political correctness, indoor smoking bans, system reforms or anything else instigated by governments nowadays – has nothing to do with caring for us or our planet and everything to do with controlling us more.

All in all, I certainly don't live a lifestyle all that geared up to what people usually regard as green principles.

I won't be standing for election, marching with a placard, joining committees, attending public meetings or taking any kind of direct action. I shall stay firmly in the shadows, happy to pay subscriptions to the Green Party and vote for its candidates.

But I do avidly advocate treasuring our environment – our lifeline - and curtailing activities that harm or destroy it.

And I zealously support most of the comments and aspirations of green activists. I back and donate cash to charities like Friends of the Earth, WSPA and the WWF.

But, contrary to popular myth, the Greens aren't just a bunch of idealistic tree-huggers. There's a heck of a lot more to them than that.

Yes, they're very hot on environmental issues. Always have been, always will be. Caring for the planet is central to their vision.

But they're just as passionate about looking after people. They demand social justice and real democracy – redistributing wealth and power far more equally and fairly.

And it's this aspect of their campaigning that especially appeals to me. They're saying the things that socialists and liberals should be – and in fact used to, quite loudly, before tasting power and being exposed as so depressingly like the Tories.

I love the democratic nature of the Greens worldwide – different sectors in different places emphasizing different aspects of pressing issues facing humanity and our Earth. Debate is encouraged and there's no blind adherence to rigid party lines.

Greens come from the right, left and centre of the political spectrum. Some are hard line ecologists, others spring from the radical left, some from the conservative fringes and others still are anarchists.

But, taken as a whole, their policies and ideals overlap and accord with my own time and time again - more regularly than any other political party. That's why they have my support and my vote from now on.

Or at least until they show themselves to be as devious, power-mad and unscrupulous as other politicians. I really, really hope they don't.

Okay, granted - no political system is perfect and not one has all the answers. Just like the organised religions. But at least some are better at asking the right questions. They have their priorities more correctly sorted.

And the Greens welcome diversity and discussion where others firmly discourage it.

October 13 – Have I gone completely mad? - Quite possibly. Do I care? – Not really. La la la.

October 14 – Wishing a very happy birthday to my good friend Christine, as in Tom and Chris. I don't have her mobile number so I text Tom to send my best wishes to her this morning.

During our brief text conversation, he sent me their address so I could post signed copies of Sunshine and Ice volumes one and two to him. I'll do the same with the rest of my books when they're published.

He made a wisecrack about me now being an "international author" – ha ha, not quite mate!

In fact, I'm a long way off being a smash-hit success, and in truth I'm not that sure I'd want to have that high a profile anyway.

I've given away more copies of my books than have been sold at the moment. But then, my mates have all been really nice and supportive – and if each of them tells just five people, and those people buy them, it'll start the ball rolling.

Besides, being rich and famous never was the aim of the exercise – though making money from my crazy writings would be a nice bonus, especially if it's enough to ensure I have no financial worries from now on. A dream, probably, but a cool one!

October 15 – I watched an old episode of the superb TV detective drama series Inspector George Gently yesterday evening. If you've not seen it, Martin Shaw plays the title character, a Northern copper back in the 1960s when the times really were a changing fast.

Last night's programme centred on racial tension between white and black people at the time of Enoch Powell's famously inflammatory "rivers of blood" speech.

I could not help thinking how topical this storyline was. Seems to me that Muslims, the Polish, Romanians and others are now being subjected to similarly disgusting hate campaigns as black citizens were then.

It really is depressing as hell to realise that, after that tidal wave of social change in the sixties and seventies, things have now reverted in some areas to the horrible way they were beforehand - in the bad old days.

And I'm deeply saddened that friends and acquaintances of mine – people I consider decent, kind and reasonable folk – are among those slating those from other cultures and nationalities and telling cruel jokes about them. That sucks!

But then, if you go back to the sixties and seventies, racial and sexual discrimination were seen as perfectly normal and natural. Most of us showed at least traces of them and no-one considered it a big deal – apart from black or female victims of course.

Such attitudes were ingrained in the fabric of our culture. The targets have changed but the mindset is identical.

Which brings me to an item on the news this morning about English schoolchildren now being taught Cantonese as a second language.

This seems decidedly strange to me and will take some getting used to, but apparently it's being done because of China's rise as a superpower and its growing connections and influence in the west.

Learning French, German, Italian or Spanish seems a lot more logical to me as they're much closer neighbours and there's been a lively exchange of citizens and trade between us and them for centuries.

I suppose you could add Portuguese, Polish, Russian, Indian, Pakistani and Romanian to that list – it makes more sense to learn these languages, as people speaking them are here in droves already and have been for a long time.

But Chinese? And why not Japanese? Both seem light years removed from what's traditionally taught in our classrooms.

I guess the powers that be will say they're looking to the future. But this new turn of events will no doubt get the hard line English bigots in a right old lather.

Makes you wonder if the politicians and the newsmen are pushing this Chinese angle deliberately, to play the Enoch Powell card yet again, ignite fury and raise even more suspicion and hatred towards people of different races and cultures.

In other words, it looks uncannily like another classic example of our old friend divide and rule, taking us to new heights – or should that be depths? – Of hostility and intolerance.

It's a well known fact that I detest racism and see it as totally illogical and just plain daft, given my all-embracing worldview.

But, watching Inspector George Gently last night, I had an unsettling thought. What if someone close to me had been killed or maimed by a person from a different cultural or racial background? Would I think differently?

I sincerely hope not. But the truth is, I don't know. And that, in a nutshell, is why racial tension and its casualties are so corrosive, counterproductive and dangerous to each and every one of us.

It makes peace and love far more than just a vague hippie mantra. Promoting both is vital, practical common sense for the future of mankind.

And the planet, too. For in exploring the Green alternative afresh, I see that this is another reason why I find the philosophies of Saint Francis of Assisi, William Blake, Percy and Mary Shelley, Gandhi, Aldous Huxley, John Ruskin, Martin Luther King and William Morris so attractive.

All of them advocated respect for both people and their environment, taking a holistic approach to humankind and our place in the natural order of things.

And we can add to that list certain politicians like German Green activist Petra Kelly and Bolivian President Evo Morales, who in 2008 gave a speech outlining his ten commandments for better living.

They encapsulated a holistic view of how things should be – putting care for Earth and all its citizens at the heart of policy making.

Petra Kelly said environmental damage was already critical and time was running out for us all. We had to apply the brakes as a matter of urgency.

She issued the stark warning: "If we don't do the impossible, we shall be faced with the unthinkable."

Kelly was killed in mysterious circumstances in 1992. Police said she was shot dead while sleeping. But her influence lives on and thrives among Green thinkers.

Gandhi astutely observed that the planet provides enough for everyone's need but not everyone's greed. And Karl Marx advocated respect for nature, saying we were not Earth's owners – merely stewards, looking after it for future generations.

And let's not forget the good old Dalai Lama - a simply wonderful human being who speaks more divine wisdom than anyone else alive about how we should treat each other and our surroundings with care and compassion.

I could fill a book with his enlightened quotations. No doubt people already have.

This brilliantly-inspired guru's all-encompassing message of kindness is a blazing beacon of light in a deeply flawed global ecosystem where humans, animals, forests and landscapes all suffer greatly from screwed-up attitudes and destructive activities.

And these are driven by the insane quest to abuse, exploit and control for short-term gain with little or no regard for the serious long-term consequences.

We should all listen and take heed of his advice. If we did this, even a little bit, our world and our lives would be transformed radically for the better.

****

CHAPTER THREE – NUTTERS

October 16 – Some people have a bucket list, but not me.

Such lists are itemised summaries of things individuals feel they must do before kicking the bucket – that is, leaving this plane of existence.

This could be anything from viewing Paris from the top of the Eiffel Tower, visiting the Pyramids, going to the World Cup finals, ballroom dancing, sky diving or appearing on a game show.

I don't have such a list. I'm far from adventurous, never have liked travelling, and feel that, whatever happens here on in, I've lived a life packed with exciting and highly enjoyable experiences.

I hold many golden memories and I'm quite content to just dawdle along in my own cosy little rut from now on, maybe taking the occasional short trip away or attending a local rock gig. I have no desire to test or challenge myself. Never did, really.

In fact, people who do amuse me. I can't understand why they feel they have to deliberately put their bodies and emotions through the wringer, making themselves feel stressed and uncomfortable. What's the point? Anything for an easy life I say.

A very good friend of mine recently seemed surprised when I said I'd realised a dream by getting my books published. She said there was a lot more to life and she feared I was somehow missing out.

Maybe for another person that wouldn't suffice. Some folk are obsessed with new experiences, the more outlandish, the better. Others are adrenalin junkies, thriving on danger. Sod that!

I have no such compulsion. And I fear it's them that have something sadly missing from their lives, not me – otherwise they'd be content with what they've got.

At the risk of sounding dull and boring, I have no wish to break out of my comfort zone. I'm quite happy here, thanks very much. And I certainly don't feel I'm denying myself in any way.

Life in the bus lane suits me just fine. I have my family and friends whom I love dearly. I can still party, laugh and have a good time. That's enough for me.

And I can go anywhere I like, free of charge, in my head, using my imagination while staying safe and sound in my own armchair.

Would my attitude change if I were told I had a limited time left? Possibly, but I doubt it. There might be a fresh urgency to get certain things done, but that would be on a strictly personal level, not involving exotic locations or new experiences.

So I don't have a bucket list. And I'm someone who's always writing lists.

What to do each day, my top 100 bands and albums, what food and provisions to buy at the shops, which clothes to pack if I do go away for a short break, what music CDs I want to get my hands on, and so on. I love lists.

October 16 – later – I've just had a fab few hours with my very good buddy Jem Hannen, at pubs and his home, involving lager, food, and silliness. Plus of course Jem's speciality - brandy coffee. Nice!

Our mutual dear mate Steve Yarwood was supposed to be joining us but he cried off at the last minute because he wasn't well. Such a shame, especially as he missed out on our "jolly boys" Weymouth day trip last November through ill health, too.

At some point the three of us will have a few hours together to relax, enjoy each others' company and have fun – like we used to. I hope and pray it's soon.

But it was so good to spend time with Jem - a close and treasured friend - plus his girlfriend Debs, his brothers Tony and Steve and their lovely mum.

October 17 – Hot on the heel of the kids learning Cantonese issue comes the equally startling news of moves to let Chinese firms invest in the UK nuclear power industry and maybe even have controlling stakes in future.

What makes this staggering is the glaring inconsistency it highlights in government policy-making.

So, if I've got this right, Parliament has been asked to go to war – again - with a country thousands of miles away over so-called "weapons of mass destruction" when there's scant evidence it poses any danger to us if even if it has them.

Yet we're willing to let another foreign power exercise a major influence in our own potentially apocalypse-creating nuclear resources right here in our own back yard.

And that power is China – not all that long ago seen as a very real threat to us and others, a diabolical menace hell bent on oppressive world domination.

China under Chairman Mao was often mentioned in the same breath as the old USSR was before both iron-fist communist regimes were dismantled and, on the face of it at least, replaced by democracy.

If our glorious leaders are now seemingly as paranoid about Syria as they were about China, Russia and then Iraq, how the heck does that square with turning a blind eye to the risk of other countries creating mayhem on our own soil?

For that possibility is there, and has been for years as more and more foreign powers have invested in our economy, exerting a growing influence on our lives.

Arguably, the likelihood of a back-door hostile take-over is a far more serious threat than any posed by countries and events in far-flung regions of the globe.

I must stress here that I've never had anything against the Chinese, Russians or any other group of foreigners. And I'm not suggesting for one moment that they actually have evil designs on our fair land.

I'm not that paranoid and besides, there's no evidence. But we can't forever rule out that slim possibility. And when considering nuclear power, we are talking long-term.

Having said that, it's the politicians and media folk who seem to switch from trust to suspicion and back again over other nations - not me.

In my view, they place a lot of faith in certain people but none at all in others. Then change their minds. I guess we just have to assume that the Chinese interest in us is benign, the motives purely economic and the results will be beneficial.

No point in losing sleep over it.

But it does sadden me that we can't seem to manage on our own without help from abroad in funding our industries and services, providing cash and jobs.

Another item on today's news highlighted assertions that securing paid work doesn't guarantee an escape from poverty. Really? – tell us something we don't know, Sherlock!

Or, better still; say it louder so government ministers can't pretend they haven't heard.

Many congrats to Wimbledon champion Andy Murray, who today received his OBE.

In world news, at least 93 people have died in an earthquake in the Philippines while six individuals have perished in a gas explosion in Mexico.

And in Japan, rescuers have worked through the night seeking survivors of Typhoon Wipha. The death toll currently stands at 18 but more than 50 are still missing.

October 20 – Our world is full of apparently crazy people spouting bizarre and quite unbelievable theories. Readers of my books might consider me to be one of them.

I accept that some of my views and statements may seem strange.

In particular, my opinion that dark, sinister, individuals are trying their hardest to run the whole show from the shadows, pulling everyone's strings and using smoke and mirrors, confusion and bitter division to manipulate us all to their own warped ends.

But I'm far from alone in that belief. It ties in with the widely-held assertion that a group called the Illuminati has actually been in charge for millennia, hell-bent on ruling the planet for all time for the benefit of its members and the detriment of the rest of us.

Royal bloodlines dating from ancient Sumeria and Egypt to the present day are often mentioned in this context.

It's said that policies are decided behind closed doors by unelected councils with innocuous-sounding names like the Bilderberg Group, Round Table, Safari Club and Committee of 300. They are then implemented by our official leaders.

An all powerful elite is said to work through secretive organisations such as the Freemasons and Skull and Bones Society.

The theory also links in with claims that some disturbed and dangerous individuals in positions of great power are determined to usher in a so-called New World Order of brutal control in a global fascist state.

I know this all sounds pretty far-fetched, but – at the risk of being lumped in with those regarded as deluded paranoid conspiracy theory nutters, I do accept the possibilities up to a point.

But some go far, far further, into decidedly weird and quite terrifying territory. They claim these shady characters have a different DNA to the rest of us, alien in origin and reptilian in nature.

There are even allegations of blood-guzzling Satanists using black magic, human sacrifice and paedophilia in twisted rituals behind closed doors.

Phew! Outlandish or what? Like most people, I find these last two ideas especially hard to stomach, so far removed are they from the reality we're asked to accept.

But I keep my mind flexible and receptive to all manner of explanations, concepts and scenarios. To paraphrase a famous quotation, there are more things in heaven and earth than we could ever fully comprehend.

And if we're considering bizarre, unbelievable theories, atheists would be quick to point to the one about a guy being born of a virgin, dying on a cross and then being resurrected.

On the face of it, this really does sound ridiculous - yet millions have no qualms about taking it as gospel truth without question. Incredible, don't you think? But that's what happens when metaphysics are involved and deep symbolism is taken literally.

I'm in no way dismissing supernatural forces or the power of magic. Certainly not – I'm sure both are very real. I'm just saying that we can all be pretty damned selective and irrational in what we choose to take on board and what we don't.

I've said it before and I'll say it again - keep an open mind, continue to ask questions and never accept anything you're told at face value without carefully analysing it first. Then, and only then, decide if it rings true and feels right.

But even after all that, we can still get it spectacularly wrong. We're only human. But hopefully we learn from experience as new evidence presents itself to challenge our paradigms – in other words, as life's unexpected twists and turns keep us on our toes.

October 21 – For those puzzled by my frequent references to those on high trying to control us, here's a statistic to get your head around.

Apparently, there's one CCTV camera for every 11 people in the UK, making us the most watched population on the planet.

Our caring, trustworthy leaders would have us believe this is for the benefit of us all, helping to ensure our safety and security.

But I see a far more sinister form of security at work here. A security based on relentless surveillance and intrusive control.

I'm fully aware that there's actually a massive irony in what I'm saying. I cannot dispute that a CCTV device at the site where I was assaulted in 2001 could well have saved me many months of hassle and a day trip to Bristol to fight for justice.

I would have probably received the full amount of compensation I was entitled to without question – not half of it after a lot of grief.

So, on a purely personal level, I must accept that such a camera might have done me a big favour.

That said, I still assert that this would have been a beneficial side-effect of a generally unsettling bid to watch our every move and keep us monitored and in line.

No doubt some would say it could combat terrorism and crime, adding that if we're behaving ourselves we have nothing to worry about. True – but I still seriously question the motives behind the surveillance culture. It still makes me uneasy.

CCTV equipment is the most obvious sign of this bid to control us more and more.

Then there are speed cameras – often seen as a cynical bid to amass cash rather than a genuine attempt to promote road safety.

And let's not forget micro-chips.

At present we're seeing a growing trend of chipping family pets – widely accepted as a good thing if it prevents Kitty or Fido getting lost or stolen.

But there are claims this is just a stepping-stone to the wholesale micro-chipping of humans at birth.

This downright shocking idea would also be presented as beneficial, since the chip would carry details such as parentage, blood type and other useful data.

But the first question that I and other similarly alarmed people would ask is what additional sensitive personal information would these chips also contain?

And could the practice of chipping open the back door to the planting of other tiny technological wonders in our heads or bodies programmed to directly control us?

Science fiction, pure fantasy or frightening near-future fact? - You decide!

But don't listen to me – I'm just a fruit loop with some very strange ideas.

October 22 – An item on today's TV news said the government was proposing to charge foreign visitors for using our National Health Service, to prevent what it describes as "healthcare tourism."

The politicians are saying that such people should pay into our system for at least a year before being entitled to free medical and surgical services.

But this seems unduly harsh to me.

Depending on the details, I might actually support – up to a point - their similar plans to halt so-called "benefit tourism" by refusing certain welfare payments to some guests from overseas for the same amount of time.

But I would need to be absolutely sure that saving cash was necessary, and my all-important rider would be to treat each case on its merits, preventing undue hardship. I know, I know – it's one of my favourite mantras. But I feel with very good reason.

The way is see it, with-holding benefits from healthy, able-bodied foreigners showing a reckless disregard for the small matter of being able to pay their way is one thing.

But to treat those needing healthcare the same is going too far. No-one asks for medical or surgical assistance for fun, unless they're downright weird. To turn them away if they can't pay seems decidedly cruel.

Once again, I'm deeply suspicious about the thinking behind such proposals. Saving money is one thing – if it's actually necessary, and I'm far from convinced it is.

But cutting costs, or making extra cash, by penalising those in need of handouts, services or healthcare is just plain wrong.

If cuts are required – and that's a massive if – then take money from those who have fortunes and could easily spare a few grand, not people struggling to make ends meet.

I'm with Gandhi on this one – our world has sufficient resources for everyone's need, but not their greed. Redistribution of wealth is desperately overdue.

And, when all's said and done, no matter what our leaders tell us, saving cash isn't the real reason for their cutbacks and clampdowns anyway. That's just the cover story.

It's actually all about stirring up distrust and hatred for those perceived as outsiders while also creating friction between different sections within our communities.

In other words, playing a dangerous game of divide and rule and keeping us all wary of each other, unsettled and fractious, therefore so damned easy to scare and control. That's the real purpose for the cuts that are causing such widespread misery and rage.

The same applies to government policy-making no matter who's in charge. The Conservatives are just more blunt, blatantly callous and obnoxious, that's all.

Is this crazy talk? Take another look around you and then tell me I'm wrong. I'd actually love it if you could persuade me that I am. It would be a relief.

But until then, I'll carry on suspecting the worst of our political leaders, be they from the ranks of the blue, red or orange brigades.

October 28 – I detest rain and usually try to avoid it. But yesterday evening I braved torrential downpours to attend a gig. And boy was it worth it!

Hawklords were playing at The Anvil, a new rock bar in Holdenhurst Road, Bournemouth. And they were superb.

Formed among former members of Hawkwind, their music is in the same kind of psychedelic, hypnotic, spacey groove.

And it was a very intimate session indeed with few spectators in a tiny venue.

But that didn't stop the musicians putting on one hell of a performance. Sweet!

I got home buzzing and went on Facebook to report my joyful experience – only to find sombre tributes to rock star Lou Reed, who had died earlier that day, aged 71.

A founder-member of the brilliant and influential Velvet Underground, Reed then went on to carve a highly-respected solo career.

His excellent songs included Walk on the Wild Side, Perfect Day, and Venus in Furs, Sweet Jane, Heroin and Waiting for my Man.

He was a rock and roll icon, brave in his choice of subject matter and highly inventive in his approach to writing and performing. He will be sorely missed but his music will live on and continue to inspire new generations.

October 28 – later – The heavy rains I weathered last night were part of a major storm that hit southern England, causing havoc and killing four people. Our thoughts are with their families and friends.

October 30 – Well, it's that time of year again when we get inundated with plaintive requests for money from a host of charities.

There are so many of them nowadays that it's really difficult deciding who should get our spare cash – if indeed we have any. They're all worthy causes reliant on funding to continue with their vital beneficial work.

I think it's really cool that, after many years struggling on benefits, I've recently been restored to a position where I've been able to donate to such organisations again – albeit through tragic circumstance. And I do so in my dear sister's memory.

Like most folk, I've especially picked the charities I've had direct contact with – such as Macmillan Cancer Care and the British Heart Foundation.

I've also supported the Royal Bournemouth and Southampton Hospitals as thank-yous for their sterling work caring for me when I had my cardiac crises. And Arthritis Care has received donations in recognition of my dodgy hip.

My mum had developed Alzheimer's by the time she died of cancer so I've also given to the Alzheimer's Society. And my dad suffered all his life with psoriasis – a nasty skin condition – so I've helped the Psoriasis Association as well.

I'm a keen supporter of Strummerville, the organisation set up in rock star Joe Strummer's memory to give disadvantaged but talented musicians and artists crucial assistance by introducing them to useful and sympathetic contacts in these fields.

And, like most people, I buy Big Issues from street vendors and Remembrance Day poppies from shops.

For the rest, I try to spread it evenly across the board - including Age UK, Great Ormond Street Children's Hospital, Cancer Research, the Blue Cross animal charity, Help for

Heroes, Amnesty International, Water Aid, Friends of the Earth and WSPA.

I'm not saying this to blow my own trumpet – I'm just using examples while giving name checks to a number of very worthy causes doing excellent work. Others will have their own reasons to support different charities, or be too skint to be able to.

I'm really trying to make two points here. One is that it's great that I've been able to donate after so long of having to be unwillingly but necessarily stingy.

The second is that it's such a massive shame we have to be so selective and we can't donate to all the charities needing our help.

October 31 – Happy Halloween guys! Tonight's the night for spooky costume parties and trick or treating – the fun aspects of an ancient religious festival with its roots firmly planted in England's old belief system before Christianity arrived here.

Wiccans, Druids and followers of other nature faiths call it Samhain, and for them it's an important fire festival and a crucial turning point in the cycle of the seasons.

It's a magical, mystical time when the wall separating our world from the next is at its thinnest, providing us with the most effective opportunity to cross between the two

For pagans, it's a sacred occasion steeped in history and tradition – a chance to re-connect with Mother Earth in a profound and spiritual way.

Christians also celebrate it – for them, today is All Hallows Eve and tomorrow, November 1st, All Hallows' Day, or to give it's more modern title, All Saints' Day.

November 1 – It's Friday today, and what a week it's been, full of strange but very pleasant coincidences.

On Sunday and Tuesday, I had text conversations with my old pal Tom Jones – my long time bro and my best man when I got wed.

During our short exchange, Tom told me that our mutual buddy Steve Gray had just become a dad again at the age of 53. Nice one Steve, I thought, haven't seen you for years mate, wonder what you're up to and how you're getting on.

On Wednesday, Tom's sister Carole, a dear and cherished friend, got in touch by Facebook suggesting we swapped phone numbers to help ensure we stayed in contact – a suggestion I responded to straightaway by replying with my mobile details.

Then, floor me with a feather, yesterday afternoon I sat down at my computer and went on Facebook to find a friend request from the very same Steve Gray, one of our old "gang of four" with Tom and Andy Bethune.

Tom's not on the social network site but it seems Steve and I have a mutual FB friend in my mate John Palmer, who I still see sometimes at the Bell (Seabourne's Bar). I didn't even realise Steve and John knew each other. Small world, innit?

And as if to continue the theme, a little later yesterday I went to visit Sam Excell, who'd invited me to help her and her family celebrate Halloween at their home with our mutual friend Tina Mcauley.

I've previously explained how Sam used to baby-sit for Tom and Christine many moons ago when she was still a teenager. I didn't really know her then - it's only in recent years that we've become close. She also knows Steve, Andy and John Palmer.

****

CHAPTER FOUR – RHYMES

November 3 - Searching for an old lyric I wrote years ago, I started reading through a folder of my rock and roll rhymes.

And during this trip down memory lane yesterday, I discovered that, although decades have passed since I penned them, some were actually surprisingly topical.

So here's a selection from the period 1974 to 1993, given a bit of a makeover…

John and Sue
Martin Money December 3, 1974.

"Our love will last forever and live beyond the grave
A glimpse into the crystal life, a sacred gem to save
One day I'll be a rock star and you will be my bride
We'll climb the stardust stairway to glittered fame worldwide."

He played guitar in a rocking band that toured the local pubs
She thought her super ace of hearts would soon be king of clubs
They planned to marry in the spring with romance in their eyes
They danced through life and shrugged when told that such love sometimes dies.

*Their wedding day was blessed with sun to match their
cloudless joy
It seemed the future promised much for happy girl and boy*

*"Our love will last forever and live beyond the grave
A glimpse into the crystal life, a sacred gem to save."*

*But when our couple settled down their world began to change
No time to play in rocking bands – two lives to re-arrange
Nine to five then overtime to pay the mounting bills
A wife and babe to care for now and love is slowly killed.*

*Bored and disillusioned, his smile can shine no more
His dreams of fame and fortune lie splintered on the floor
The love runs cold inside him and turns to bitter hate
He feels he must escape this hell before it gets too late.*

One blazing row too many and John storms out the gate.

*He walks for miles, she sits and weeps – "How did it die?"
they cry
They wish they could turn back the clock, give love another
try
He wanders home, ashamed and sad, not knowing what he'll
find
But Sue sheds happy tears of joy, two loving souls entwined
They promise not to let their cares turn love deaf, dumb and
blind.*

*"Our love will last forever and live beyond the grave
A glimpse into the crystal life, a sacred gem to save."*

Freedom for the Gambler
Martin Money Dec 14-15, 1975.

I feel strange sensations taking hold of me
Ever since I took the plunge that set me free
I left the cosy comfort of routine
For the icy wastes of chance
I joined the gamblers' dance
And found out how exciting life could be.

Since I broke away from drudgery and dread
I have rediscovered peace of mind instead
I've found new friends to cultivate my joy
A feeling I belong
And once again I'm strong
My heart is bound by love's eternal thread.

Here is love, here is hope
Here is peace, fun and grace
New adventures, fresh beginnings
New horizons to embrace
Here is life, here is strength
Here is sight, sound and smell
Touching, tasting, moving, healing
Spirit's rising, feeling well.

Times like This

Martin Money July 18, 1976.

A dazzling ball of light throws prisms on the floor
With every song the deejay plays I feel a little more like a
loser

The lovers dance in pairs beneath a silver sphere
The music's slow and tender now – if only she were her, I
would choose her.

At times like this I feel it most – this yearning deep inside
A need to have her close by me – my lover, friend and bride
She would be my angel and my star, forever my star.

I came here with a friend but still I feel alone
I try my best to bring to life a heart as cold as stone- I'm a
loser.
At times like this I feel it most – this yearning deep inside
A need to have you close by me – my lover, friend and bride
You would be my angel and my star, whoever you are.

Love Burn the Ice

Martin Money Jan 5-7, 1977

Lunatics with steel and fire are roaming through the streets
A gang of school kids throwing stones at soldiers on the beat
Latent fear has gripped the town, the racketeer's moved in
He runs the war to line his purse and prospers from the sin

Hardened by the endless fight, the parents tell their young
Not to mix with aliens and so the strife goes on
Catholic or Protestant or Muslim, Jain or Jew
What's the use in talking God while killing as you do?

And so the madness spreads...

...But wait, I hear a sound
A peaceful noise, a single voice
It's crying out for peace, crying out for peace,
Crying out for peace for one and all

And now a second voice has joined the song
It's getting strong
They're crying out for peace, crying out for peace,
Crying out from both sides of the wall.

United once again, they share a common pain
Their tears of joy dissolve the wall of fear

And so the movement grows...

...Blessed be the ones who reconcile
Blessed be the ones who bring a smile
Blessed be the ones who face the fire of anger, ice of hate
Love burn the ice.

Blades and Anvils

Martin Money April 27-May 6, 1977

Get out the anvil, stoke up the fire
Go fetch the hammer, build up the pyre
You're trying to beat me until I fit your mould
Red for the workers, blue for the boss
Make up you mind- don't argue the toss
And don't waste your time searching too long for the gold.

This blade don't want to be blunted, this flame don't want to die
This rock's gotta do some rolling; this dog is refusing to lie.

Sick of the boredom, tired of the lies
Of those who are trying to cover my eyes
They're killing my hope but my spirit's still alive
Red for the workers, blue for the boss
Make up your mind, don't argue the toss
Or fritter your time till the carrion crows arrive.

This blade don't want to be blunted, this flame don't want to die
This rock's gotta do some rolling; this dog is refusing to lie.

Don't stab my heart, don't make it scream
Don't sink my ship, don't steal my dream
Don't quench my blaze, don't bleed me dry
Don't write me off, don't tear my sky
Don't bury me before I'm dead
No garbage gonna fill my head
No concrete gonna hold me in
No system gonna stop my pen
This rock's still got some rolling left to do
This dog's still got some life before he's through.

74

Hate on your Doorstep

Martin Money Aug 9-14, 1977.

When I see so much trouble, so much strife
It makes me want to cry – yeah cry
When I see so much anger, so much pain
You know it's such a shame -real shame

The pictures on the TV screen – they break my heart so
constantly
I know it's just a hundred miles away
The tragedy of civil war, the front-line's by your own front
door
It seems to get a little worse each day.

When I see all the people killed in vain
It's such a deadly game – who's to blame?
When I see all the fear that leads to war
The writing's on the wall – heed the call.

I saw it on my TV screen – I had to gaze on helplessly
A techni-colour nightmare edged with pain
The commentator seemed to cry, a glint of moisture round his
eye
The same old sorry story yet again.

Hate on your doorstep, blood on your carpet, tears in your
eyes
Naked aggression by your own people under your skies
Enough to make you cry - yeah cry.

You Keep Me Sane

Martin Money March 7-8, 1988.

So I'm caught in this trap – people say it is one of my making
But I can't recollect having asked for this grave undertaking
I accept I have failed to take chances that came- yes I missed them
Now I'm hung out to dry like a lamb being fed to the system.
Though I'm stuck in this hole it's a blessing to be here with you
You're the reason I live – the incentive I need to pull through
You're the one who keeps me sane as you take away the pain
Like the sun dispels the rain you help me, help me, help me take the strain.

If I shattered the mould, came out fighting for gold, would I get it?
If I took all the risks would I only survive to regret it?
If I altered my course, set my face to the wind, would I perish?
It's a gamble so big playing poker with all that you cherish.

If I made up my mind to climb out of this rut would I lose you?
If I tried to explain would it make you upset or confuse you?
If I gritted my teeth, started over again, would you follow?
If I made it alone any victory won would be hollow.

Though I'm stuck in this hole it's a blessing to be here with you
You're the reason I live – the incentive I need to pull through
You're the one who keeps me sane as you take away the pain
Like the sun dispels the rain you help me, help me, help me take the strain.

We're Just Human

Martin Money Aug 2-5, 1988

What do you see when you look at me - is it the man you'd like me to be?
What do I view as I gaze at you – is it the same as you're wanting me to?

Fixed ideas are hard to shake, misconceptions tough to break
Rosy tint or sceptic's glance? – Different facets, altered stance
No one person holds the key to unlock the mystery
We're just human, yeah, we're just human.

Why do you say that I'm ill today – just coz I'm acting a diff'rent way?
Why should I care if you change your hair?
Under the skin, the same heart's beating there

Fixed ideas are hard to shake, misconceptions tough to break
Rosy tint or sceptic's glance? – Different facets, altered stance
Who is wrong and who is right? We could argue through the night
No one person holds the key to unlock the mystery
We're just human, yeah, we're just human.

Suffer the Children

Martin Money Aug 6-7, 1988

Surveying the bump on your stomach
I ponder on what it will be
A sinner, a saint or a fruitcake?
The onus lies largely with me.

Consider the child in the cradle
And wonder just what lies ahead
A life of great joy and achievements
Or one full of sadness and dread?

It's a fool who takes too lightly
The responsibility
Of bringing up these young hearts
To be happy, true and free.

These small feet will march to the future –
Or will they just march into war?
The pioneers, princes and prophets
The wise and the rich and the poor.

And what of the pressure on mothers
To give birth and not hesitate?
While others pass stern moral judgement
The baby will bear all the hate.

Revenge is Sweet

Martin Money Aug 9-12, 1988

Strike a nail into my heart, watch the red juice flow
Hammer home your twisted dreams, let your anger go
Scorch my soul with blazing hate; freeze it with your ice
Sting it with your acid tongue; squeeze it in your vice

But you'd better say your prayers before you sleep
Coz resentment in this boy is running deep
And he's gonna get you back, you'll feel the heat
Of revenge so sweet.

Smash my visions, hurt me with every dirty trick
Tear my ego into shreds, cut me to the quick

But you'd better say your prayers before you sleep
Coz resentment in this boy is running deep
And he's gonna get you back, you'll feel the heat
Of revenge so sweet.

Just coz life's turned sour for you, malice fills your days
I'm the butt of all your rage, I'm the one who pays

But you'd better say your prayers before you sleep
Coz resentment in this boy is running deep
And he's gonna get you back, you'll feel the heat
Of revenge so sweet.

Yes, you'd better say your prayers before too late
Coz the time's approaching to retaliate
Yes I'm poised to get you back, you'll feel the heat
Of revenge so sweet.

Power Junkie

Martin Money Aug 13-14, 1988.

She rules the land with an iron claw
She'll turn the screw then turn it more
She courts the rich and robs the poor
She's a power junkie.

Her courtiers must with one accord
Obey their mighty overlord
Or they will feel her brutal sword
She's a power junkie.

She's the wicked witch of your fairy tales
She's your worst nightmare, she's your seven hells
She's the power junkie.

The acid monarch's hooked on fame
In traitors' blood she'll write her name
In history she'll stake her claim
As a power junkie.

But deep inside the tyrant's lair
Her blue-eyed boy is waiting there
He'll throw her from her golden chair
He's a power junkie.

He's the evil prince of your fairy tales
He's your worst nightmare, he's your seven hells
He's a power junkie.

Tarnished

Martin Money October 17-23, 1988

*This is my land, I'll state it clearly - My native home I treasure
dearly
I love it just as much as you do – but I reject your savage
point of view*

*Our country's flag should stand for justice and shelter where
the sharing crust is
A shining badge for truth and true love – but in your hands I
see it drenched in blood.*

*You steal the name of this proud nation and damn its soul
through degradation
You take up arms when others cross you and fail to see they
love their countries too.*

*You can't stand those who aren't your kind or from a foreign
land
You hate the ones who speak in tongues you cannot understand
You say to hold our heads up high we must make enemies
You won't accept that diff'rent shades make dazzling tapestries
Our motherland is dear to me but it's just one branch of a
bigger tree
Bigger tree, bigger tree – bigotry is all I see.*

*This is my land, I'll state it clearly - My native home I treasure
dearly
I love it still so passionately – this tarnished gem set in a
troubled sea.*

Shock Tactics

Martin Money Oct 20-23, 1988

Shock tactics will get results
A power surge, a thousand volts
A flashing blade, a stone-hard sell
A fortune paid for kiss-and-tell
Shock tactics.

She struts her stuff without a care –
That fire cat with the flame red hair
She'll trap you with her spell so neat
Then make you pay to keep her sweet.

The ripper with the bloodstained blade
Will make you wish to God you'd prayed
With violence he'll state his case
With evil glee he'll cut your face.

Shock tactics – kiss and tell
Shock tactics – wicked spell
Shock tactics – the fires of hell
Shock tactics.

Ambition's slave is cold and sharp
He's got no scruples, got no heart
He'll crush you with his steel-capped boot
Assassin in the tailored suit
Shock tactics.

Contradictions

Martin Money March 25, 1989

You're a mass of contradictions, just like me
And we cannot see our own hypocrisy.

You say you're on the breadline but there's gold upon your wrist
You pray for peace on Sundays but a fight you can't resist
You love to pay lip-service to the brotherhood on man
But when charity comes knocking you'll avoid it if you can

You can't abide fox hunting and you preach ecology
Then you put on furs and perfumes, spray the air with CFC

You're a mass of contradictions, just like me
And we cannot see our own hypocrisy.

You say all men are equal but you treat your lady cruel
You kick your dog but feel that saving whales is super-cool

You're a mass of contradictions, just like me
And we cannot see our own hypocrisy.

I Mean Business

Martin Money Feb 14-24, 1990.

I'm sick and tired of messing around
Taking the rap, making no sound
I'm out to claim what's rightly mine
I mean business.

I've been stuck in this rut and wasting time
But I've woken up to a heinous crime
I'm an angry man who's after blood
I mean business.

I mean business
Yes I mean business
From this point on
Look out world
I mean business.

I've been going mad getting used and bored
But now I want my just reward
My mind's made up – I won't give in
I mean business.

I mean business
Yes I mean business
From this point on
Look out world
I mean business.

I'll Never Forget

Martin Money March 2-6, 1990

People ask me how I feel - I tell them I'm okay
Deep inside I'm hurting still – much more than words could
say
Broken bones can mend and heal as splints are tossed aside
Broken hearts leave open wounds we feel obliged to hide.

I'll never forget, never ever forget – oh no, I'll never forget.

Babe I love you very much - it's plain for all to see
But even you cannot erase this poignant memory
Fix me with that clear blue gaze, hold my trembling hand
Light my path with loving smiles but try to understand.

I'll never forget, never ever forget – oh no, I'll never forget.

Darling, you're my morning star, you mean the world to me
But even you cannot erase this poignant memory

I'll never forget, never ever forget – oh no, I'll never forget.

Pushed Too Far

Martin Money Nov 26-Dec 1, 1990

He's lost his edge, he's lost his touch
You pushed too far, you asked too much
He's going down, he's all at sea
He's getting wild, he's just like me

And mister, you're to blame
You pressed and pressurised
You never asked him how he felt
You never read his eyes.

He's lost his nerve, he's lost his way
He's fading fast, he's had his day
You made him sweat. You made him cry
You broke his will, you bled him dry

And woman, you're to blame
You pressed and pressurised
You never asked him how he felt
You never read his eyes.

He's cracking up, he's had his fill
Your cold demands have made him ill
While in your ivory castle you couldn't give a fig
You smashed his dreams, you crushed his pride,
You snapped him like a twig.

She's lost her edge, she's lost her touch
You pushed too far, you asked too much
You made her sweat, you made her cry
You broke her will, you bled her dry.

And mister, you're to blame
You pressed and pressurised
You never asked her how she felt
You never read her eyes.

"He's cracking up, he's got a knife" –
And with a slash he took his life
While in your ivory castle you couldn't give a fig
You smashed his dreams, you crushed his pride,
You snapped him like a twig

And mister, you're to blame
You pressed and pressurised
So tell me how it feels right now –
You caused a man to die.

Dirty Tricks

Martin Money March 14-April 9, 1991

Viewing from a distance, it looks so civilised
But tranquil rural settings mask a devil in disguise
A mutilated voodoo doll drips terror from a gate
While madly-scribbled letters burn with bigotry and hate
And meanwhile, in the rest home, the body bags arrive
The innocents are scared to death – the target's still alive!

Slaughter in the city blocks or witch-hunts in the sticks
When the English have an axe to grind you can count on dirty
tricks.

The tenement's vibrating to a song of national pride
While ethnic non-conformists lock their doors and stay inside
The window glass is shattered as a missile hits the stair
A bright flame splits the darkness and there's murder in the
air

Slaughter in the city blocks or witch-hunts in the sticks
When the English have an axe to grind you can count on dirty
tricks.

Viewing from a distance, it looks so civilised
But close-knit urban settings mask a devil in disguise
Coz there's comfort in your numbers and your uniformity
But a lethal undercurrent seethes with mob mentality

Slaughter in the city blocks or witch-hunts in the sticks
When the English have an axe to grind you can count on dirty
tricks.

The Cost of Going Green
Martin Money April 24-May 15, 1991

I don't really like computers but I have to stay in touch
Don't want to join polluters but conversion costs too much

And it's a blatant crime – it's quite obscene
That only the rich can afford to be green.

The labels scream out "save the world" on high-cost merchandise
I crossed the road to Oxfam's shop – they didn't have my size
While rock and movie superstars throw lifelines to the poor
We struggle in our money pit with dreams to give much more.

And it's a blatant crime – it's quite obscene
That only the rich can afford to be green.

There's a million hungry mouths to feed, ten thousand trees to plant
I yearn to do my bit to help but bankers say I can't
Yet their banks have made a fortune on the interest we've shown
As the Third World scrapes the breadline saddled with a vicious loan

And it's a blatant crime – it's quite obscene
That only the rich can afford to be green.

There's a million hungry mouths to feed, ten thousand trees to plant
I yearn to do my bit to help but bankers say I can't
And our leaders talk recession till the next time there's a war

While a fat cat makes a killing selling poisons to the poor

And it's a blatant crime – it's quite obscene
That only the rich can afford to be green.

Golden Sunsets

Martin Money Jan 27-May 18, 1991.

You sink your pints and reminisce, the mem'ries flow so sweet
About four lads who shook the world and a club in Mathew Street
Reflection is so comfortable, the future looks so cold
Living in the past is one sure sign you're getting old

Paint those verbal pictures – a rosy tint collage
Charge your glass and chase your youth - A misty-haze montage.

You've got a millstone round your neck and cry out for relief
Coz everything's got so intense and shaken your belief

So paint those verbal pictures – a rosy tint collage
Charge your glass and chase your youth - A misty-haze montage

As golden sunsets flood your mind, a gilt-edged paradise
You block out all those winter times of tears and blood and ice
It's easy to forget the fights, the heart-aches and the strife
The lonely nights and bitter days that made up most your life

So paint those verbal pictures – a rosy tint collage
Charge your glass and chase your youth -A misty-haze montage.

You can't revive what's gone before, you have to look ahead
So steel yourself, accept the change, before you end up dead

And torch those fading pictures or throw them all away
Break the spell, forget your youth and face up to the day.

Stardust Memories

Martin Money April 4-6, 1992.

Have I told you lately I love you? – those three words mean so much
How I wanted your embrace last night, how I crave your tender touch
Fading pictures on the wall, a couple standing proud
Two hearts held by golden threads, two heads in a cloud
Whatever happened to those smiles, my love? - The dreams lie cut to shreds
Two hearts beat in different times as worry turns our heads

Absence makes the heart grow fonder, gives me pause to think
I'm standing on a crumbling cliff, I'm closer to the brink
We took so much for granted as stardust slipped away
We didn't even notice it, a little more each day
Can we please, please, please start again?

Have I told you lately I need you? I'm missing you so much
Did I act the fool and make you cry? – Babe, I feel so out of touch
Fading pictures on the wall, a symbol of our dreams
Something vanished down the years, left us lost, it seems.

Whatever happened to those dreams my love? – inside, they're still alive
But outside forces burst their seams – they need to be revived
Absence makes the heart grow fonder, makes me contemplate
I'm keen to make amends, my love – don't tell me it's too late

My nerves are raw and bleeding, I guess that yours are too
I'm pleading, can we heal the wounds – together, see it through?
Can we please, please, please start again?

Happy Never After

Martin Money Dec1992-Jan 1993.

Do you believe in happiness? – I'll tell you I did once
Star-spangled nights and sunny days, my life shone on all
fronts
But then my sky was torn away, my dreams were pulled apart
The love light died and darkness fell as cold words pierced
my heart

Do you believe in fairy tales? – Well, man, they don't exist
Just when you think you've sussed the plot life takes a bitter
twist
And I found out the hardest way as hope crashed round my
ears
Those scars inside, I try to hide, will burn for many years

Happy ever after? – please don't make me laugh!
Life's a bitch and then you die – what an epitaph!

Do you believe in sacred vows? – the sickest joke of all
If you put trust in spoken words you're heading for a fall
Like footprints in the sands of time, eroded by the seas
Those sparkling words are washed away to leave just
memories

Happy ever after?– please don't make me laugh!
Life's a bitch and then you die – what an epitaph!

****

CHAPTER FIVE – ROCKETS

November 5 – Whiz bang – it's Bonfire Night. And Cameron and crew have seemingly been caught with their trousers down as the immigration controversy crackles on.

The BBC news channel this morning publicised the findings of a new survey conducted by University College, London.

It concluded that, contrary to what the politicians are claiming, newcomers to the UK since 2000 have actually made a "substantial contribution" to our economy.

Rather than being a burden, as the Prime Minister would have us believe, immigrants have in fact ploughed many billions of pounds into our system during the last 13 years while taking considerably less out of it than native Brits, says the report.

This sharply contradicts Cameron's recent comments as he pledged to clampdown on what he called benefit and healthcare "tourism."

The PM said he wanted to ensure that newcomers to our shores paid into our public purse for at least a year before being permitted to claim benefits.

He proposed a similar tightening of the rules over use of the NHS, proposing that immigrants should be charged for access to medical or surgical services if needing them within a year of arrival.

The clear implication was that foreigners were proving a significant drain on our public funds and facilities.

At the time, I said I might support the first idea up to a point, depending very much on the circumstances, but I thought the second was unduly harsh - a step too far.

But this new evidence exposes dastardly David's claims for what they were – very misleading, at least exaggerated and possibly even - horror of horrors - outright fibs.

Depends who you believe I suppose – an apparently impartial group of scholars from a respected seat of learning, or a bunch of politicians with a blatantly biased agenda treating foreigners with contempt and benefit claimants as some sort of enemy within.

I know where I stand – especially when this clear dislike for outsiders doesn't seem to extend to a plan to let another nation run our nuclear power industry!

How positively puzzling. How completely crazy. How annoyingly appropriate for a government that's only constant features are its cruelty, unfairness and inconsistency!

Other items on the news included growing concern over alleged unethical practices by certain loan companies, including famous ones advertised on telly.

And on the international front, we've had today's launch of India's first mission to Mars. It coincides with that country's celebration of Diwali, a religious festival among Hindus and Jains where a central theme is fireworks, echoing our own activities at this time of year.

I find it astonishingly ironic that a country where millions starve and die in poverty and squalor can somehow find the cash to send a rocket into space – and a very big, exceedingly expensive, high-tech one at that, not the smaller firework kind!

But returning to the theme of treating foreigners with suspicion, we're just about to mark a very sombre occasion where our thoughts turn to the immense human cost of escalating conflict to extreme levels.

We consider in particular two glowing, massive, and blood-drenched examples of where this particular mindset can ultimately and terrifyingly lead.

I refer, of course, to Remembrance Sunday and the two World Wars.

As a pacifist, I detest violence but accept that in extreme cases it might be necessary, as in protecting our families or country from serious harm.

At a national level, I back the concept of strong, well-equipped armed forces devoted to this end. And I mourn the dead and support the maimed in any conflict our governments get them embroiled in, no matter how unnecessarily.

Linked to this could be a limited role for spies, merely to keep a watch that other countries aren't making plans or up to activities that would impact negatively on us.

But I feel very strongly that when it comes to defence, the clue has to be in the name.

Our military personnel should be employed in shielding us from aggressors posing a real threat to us right here, where we are - not spuriously being sent out to take part in armed struggles many miles away that wouldn't otherwise involve or endanger us.

If all nations took this view, no-one would invade or threaten anyone else so none of the armed forces would be needed anyway. How fantastic would that be?

But who's brave enough to be the first to disarm, and possibly leave themselves wide open to attack? - Ah, well there's the rub.

I suppose the answer is to keep those military organisations in place anyway – just in case. But to have a mutual agreement not to use them for aggression.

We've apparently all been trying to do this since World War Two – some more successfully than others. But certain rascals have turned invaders and spoiled things.

There's an added huge problem if, in the past – or even quite recently - you've been the ones doing the invading. That's when it gets real messy!

I suggest the answer is for everyone to learn from history, draw a line under it and pledge to live peacefully side by side from now on – only having armed forces for the purposes of protection.

November 6 – Earlier today, I was at the Royal Bournemouth Hospital for my annual heart check-up with Dr Adrian Rozkovec, my cardiac consultant. I've been told he's one of the top guys in his field in Europe.

He once again gave me the all clear and said he'd see me same time next year. Walking away, I breathed a massive sigh of relief.

Getting home, I put the kettle and telly on. I've just been watching Prime Minister's question time, being broadcast live from the House of Commons.

And I witnessed an unruly rabble of arrogant, ignorant, childish and aggressive morons barking and howling at each other like wild animals.

It was like an upper-crust version of the Jeremy Kyle Show. Part of me wished the Gunpowder Plot had succeeded in ridding us of this festering monument to deception, hypocrisy and privilege.

Only kidding, mind – or am I?

Seriously, though, I sometimes wonder how different life in out country would be if the plotters we demonise on Bonfire Night had actually managed the blow up the Houses of Parliament.

Of course, as someone who opposes violence, I would not support any use of it to achieve change. But change is badly needed and long overdue.

In my heart I've always been a rebel, a subversive – even though I haven't always shown it. I don't see how anyone with an ounce of common sense or compassion could possibly support maintenance of the status quo.

Let's face it; the whole set-up is riddled with division, inequality, corruption and injustice. Trouble is, some folk with immense power and unbridled greed have a vested interest in keeping it so.

But planting bombs and taking up arms aren't the ways to bring about change. Killing and maiming other citizens makes you just as bad and brutal as the system you're fighting against. It's destructive, counter-productive, and continues a spiral of misery.

Some wise soul once said you don't fight for peace, you peace for peace.

No, we must strive to alter things using the democratic process, working from within to promote a radical re-think of how we treat each other and the rest of creation.

This is not to say returning to the dark ages of primitive living. There's absolutely nothing wrong with cutting edge technology, just so long as it's not used in ways that harm communities, wildlife or the environment.

I don't oppose capitalism per se – just the harsh, cash-obsessed form of it we have at the moment. In fact, I firmly believe there is such a thing as compassionate capitalism, and I also hold that, with major and vital changes in emphasis, it could be employed to make the world a fairer, greener place.

And a large part of those changes would be the integration of the finer qualities of both socialism and liberalism – respect for human rights, equality, justice and peace.

In other words, furthering unity and healing the fractures and open wounds in society that are aggravated by politics as we know them. We need a new kind of politics, a total overhaul of perception, a far more spiritual and caring attitude.

This is precisely why I've joined the Green Party - to support and promote a holistic mindset whereby care for people and the planet are at the core of decision-making - and it's placed in the people's hands at a far more localised level.

You know, truly democratic.

We have to halt globalisation and the obsession with massive impersonal retail and business concerns, multi-national corporations, gigantic networks and huge political entities like the European Union.

We should be reviving a more grass-roots approach by supporting neighbourhood enterprise and talent, using locally-owned shops, trades folk and service suppliers, encouraging small businesses and buying goods made by people in our areas.

And more decision-making should be given back to district councils.

All this would help reverse the centralisation of political and economic power while replacing crude numbers games with good old-fashioned community spirit. It would also help combat pollution from long-distance lorries, planes and so on.

Of course, we could still have international trading links, political agreements and worldwide initiatives to combat climate change and other environment-saving or humanitarian measures.

But democratic and financial power should start at the bottom and work to the top – not the other way around, as currently seems to be the case.

We need a revolution for sure - but not a violent, bloodstained clash replacing one oppressive system with another.

It would have to be a revolution in thinking ushering in a new, more spiritual, nurturing and tolerant society. And it could only work if it started within us. We have to change our own perceptions before we can change our world.

Quite a challenge, really, but one we must urgently face for all our sakes. And just imagine the wonderful transformation that could result – real progress towards a better future for the first time in known history.

Now that, my friends, would be super cool.

November 7 – I have a theory, and it's this. We're all mad, some more than others, but the nature of our madness differs from person to person.

We all have our irrational traits, inexplicable fears, hang-ups, blind spots and other mental quirks and inconsistencies.

Some forms of this madness are endearing, funny and harmless. Others are ugly, unhinged and potentially lethal.

It's largely the luck of the draw which type of mental instability shows up in our words and actions.

Take me, for example. By now, you might well have concluded that I'm completely bonkers. I don't mind at all – just so long as you consider me innocuous, not dangerous. Others could feel the same – or maybe not.

But beware the person who thinks they're perfect, okay or normal – whatever that's supposed to mean. For such an individual is possibly the most damaged, deluded, deranged and dangerous of all, because they refuse to accept their own limitations.

November 9 – Remembrance Sunday, and I've been watching the London Cenotaph ceremony live on TV. When, oh when, will the wars and bloodshed stop?

But, as a stark reminder that it's not only armed conflict that claims lives, we have the shocking news that more than 10,000 people are feared dead in the Philippines after a massive typhoon destroyed homes, schools and an airport.

Kinda puts our own petty gripes about the weather into perspective somewhat.

Of course, our hearts always go out to the families and friends when citizens here actually do perish in violent storms, but thankfully that's not all that often at present – or at least until climate change starts taking its toll.

Shadow Man

Martin Money Nov 9-11, 2013.

Your lips are smiling but there's sadness in your eyes
A wistful longing that you simply can't disguise
A sign of living and clear proof you're getting old
Your mem'ry fails you as your bones ache in the cold

You're asking where the years went – lost in space
While stars you idolised all fall from grace
Your friends passed over and your fam'ly too
You wonder why they had to and not you

So you've gotta make the most of it
Do it while you can
Coz times are coming soon
When you'll be just a shadow man.

The days of youth and boldness sped by fast
The nights of vim and vigour didn't last
The world you see around you makes no sense
As crazy leaders force you off the fence

They lay down poppy wreaths – it makes you sick
Division dogs that never miss a trick
It's going just the way they had it planned
So buckle up, it's time to take a stand

And you've gotta make the most of it
Do it while you can
Coz times are coming soon
When you'll be just a shadow man.

Frost and Fire

Martin Money November 13, 2013.

I survived the frost and fire to come out the other side
But companions weren't so lucky - some were damaged,
others died
I need to count my lucky stars and live a life that suits
Not waste my time with hassle, stress or licking others' boots

Yes it's now or never, sun or storm or snow -
Just wish I'd had the courage years ago.

I'll assist the poor and needy in the ways I feel I can
Help the sick and disenfranchised and support my fellow man
Coz we must reverse the process, put a stop to greed and hate
Ditch the cruelty, bring compassion or the pain will not abate

Yes it's now or never, sun or storm or snow -
Just wish we'd had the courage years ago.

I passed through the cut glass valley where the going got so
hard
It's high time that I made amends for reckless disregard
I've spent so many decades lost in triviality
Dragged down by pointless labours that obscured the sky
from me

Coz it's now or never, sun or storm or snow -
Just wish I'd had the courage years ago.

November 22 – Wishing a very happy birthday to my son, Phil, who's 24 today. I sent him a text and wrote on his Facebook timeline this morning, having popped some money in a card and posted it to him the other day. He thanked me for them when he replied to my text.

Needless to say, I love him to bits. I would anyway, of course, but especially as for many years now he's been the main person keeping me from going under when my world has been at its darkest and craziest.

I've also had fantastic support from other family members and some brilliant close friends, but Phil's been the constant for the last quarter century.

And now I have his children – my lovely grandkids – to put a smile on my face too. I'm so lucky to have such a loving and supportive family and I really feel for those who are either alone and isolated or have families torn apart by bitter disputes.

Mum, Dad, and, particularly in later years, big sister Jan, all showered me with love and practical assistance during their times in this plane of existence.

So has Carol, my surviving sister, who also celebrates her birthday this weekend – in her case, on Sunday.

She and hubby David are coming from their Selsey home next Friday for a pre-Christmas meal with Suzette and me and to exchange festive presents and cards.

Apart from being Phil's birthday, today is also the 50th anniversary of John Kennedy's assassination – a pivotal turning point in modern history.

It's fascinating to ponder how different things might have turned out for all of us had he not been shot dead on the fateful day in Dallas, Texas in 1963.

On a far lighter note, this week is also the golden anniversary of the very first appearance of Doctor Who on telly. There have been lots of programmes already marking the occasion and there's a special anniversary episode tomorrow night.

Like most fans, I can't wait.

I first started watching this iconic sci-fi classic at the tail end of the William Hartnell era, when I was 10.

Hartnell, now long gone, was the first actor to play the time and space hopping alien but I really got hooked when his successor, the late, great Patrick Troughton, took over the role.

I also loved Jon Pertwee – also sadly no longer with us - and then came the fourth doctor, the brilliant Tom Baker, who I feel really set the standard for others to follow. They couldn't, so as I got older I lost interest and stopped tuning in.

But I became a fan all over again many years later when they revamped and re-launched the show with a millennium special starring Paul McGann followed by a new series with Christopher Eccleston playing the lead.

This was a smart, stylish re-invention of the programme that introduced us to one of the doctor's most popular travelling companions ever – Rose Tyler, played superbly by former pop star Billie Piper.

She kept the role as Eccleston gave way to David Tennant – who I feel was right up there with Tom Baker in the "best doctor" stakes. Eccleston was great, but Tennant was better.

And fans had a real treat when Tennant and Piper hooked up with Elisabeth Sladen, reviving her role as Sarah Jane Smith – the time lord's other great female companion dating back to the Jon Pertwee/Tom Baker era.

Sladen also starred in a spin-off children's series called the Sarah Jane Adventures but sadly died in 2011.

When Tennant left, we had Matt Smith – a very worthy successor but for me not quite as good.

Smith's on-screen chemistry with Karen Gillan (playing Amy Pond) was reminiscent of Tennant's with Piper.

But now it's all change again as Peter Capaldi takes over the coveted world-famous role alongside new female companion Clara Oswald, being played by Jenna Coleman.

We all wait with eager anticipation to see how they fare.

November 23 - Last night I went to another great gig at Boscombe's O2 Academy. This time it was the Black Star Riders – formed by former Thin Lizzy stalwart Scott Gorham and featuring other ex-members of that legendary band.

To say it was fantastic would be an under-statement. They did some great new material alongside many Lizzy classics including Rosalie, Emerald, Jailbreak, Southbound; the Boys are Back in Town and Whiskey in the Jar.

And they were so bloody tight – a fact made even more remarkable as it was their first date on a nationwide tour.

In short, it was another fab night of hard and heavy rock and roll in the company of my mate Carl Young, as in Sam and Carl. Nice!

November 24 – Happy birthday Carol – see you Friday.

Well, the much-anticipated Doctor Who special was everything we'd hoped for and more. Tip-top telly!

Billie Piper and David Tennant returned as the Who crew pulled out all the stops for a typically slick and clever time-hopping tale that also featured Matt Smith, Jenna Coleman and John Hurt – yes, THE John Hurt.

Even Tom Baker got in on the act with a brief appearance right at the end – a terrific bonus that had been a wonderfully well-kept secret in all the pre-broadcast publicity.

As if that wasn't enough, we also had short film clips featuring new doctor Peter Capaldi and all his predecessors in the role including Hartnell, Troughton and Pertwee – a nice touch.

It was Doctor Who at its best – funny, dramatic, sophisticated and spellbinding with a highly-inventive story line jam-packed with references to past characters and adventures.

While answering many questions raised over the years, it posed intriguing new ones to keep us enthralled. And the music and special effects were outstanding.

It was, apparently, broadcast simultaneously to more than 90 countries on six continents in 15 different languages, proving what a truly global phenomenon the programme's become. There were over 10 million viewers in the UK alone.

November 26 – Yesterday I walked into Boscombe to do a bit of shopping and collect two DVDs I had on order.

One was The Rutles – All You Need is Cash, an amazingly good parody of the Beatles story written by Monty Python star Eric Idle with songs penned by Neil Innes, formerly of the Bonzo Dog Doo Dah Band.

The Bonzos were mates of the real Beatles and featured in their film Magical Mystery Tour. And Eric was a pal of George Harrison, who not only eagerly appeared in the Rutles movie but also roped in his friends Mick Jagger and Paul Simon to take part.

Bianca Jagger, Rolling Stone Ron Wood, American comedy actors John Belushi, Dan Ackroyd and Bill Murray and fellow Python Michael Palin also star in this wonderful mickey-take-cum tribute to the original Fab Four and their entourage.

It's a genuine labour of love – obviously the work of people who deeply respect the Beatles' music, humour, attitudes and achievements.

Beautifully well observed, it's affectionate, not vicious, and an absolute treat for avid Beatle fans – for only they would get some of the jokes.

This movie is a masterpiece - satire at its very best. It's perceptive, stylish, witty and side-splittingly hilarious. And the songs are so brilliantly spot-on in their pastiche treatment of the Beatles' originals. Pure genius!

The other DVD I picked up was the Beatles' Magical Mystery Tour, which now goes in my Fab Four film collection alongside A Hard Days' Night, Help, Yellow Submarine, the Complete Anthology, Shea Stadium, Live 1966 and two discs of promos featuring them playing their greatest hits.

While food shopping in Sainsbury's during the same Boscombe trip, I snapped up two brand new music CDs – Eminem's latest album, called The Marshall Mathers LP Two, and the Best of Keane, which I'm playing as I write this.

Hearing all their prime cuts on one disc drives home just how ruddy good these guys are at coming up with melodic, catchy, inventive soft rock songs.

November 28 – I played the Eminem CD today and that's also good - okay, maybe not up to the high standard of some of his best previous work, but still well worth having in my collection.

This guy really is a mighty fine rap star. He sets his own vividly poetic, jagged and angry lyrics to music drawn from diverse sources in an irresistible aural concoction.

Yesterday, I returned to Boscombe – this time to visit a second-hand music store, where I bought a CD of live tracks from various Hawkwind shows and other discs featuring Slayer, Judas Priest, the Red Hot Chilli Peppers, Public Enemy and Cream.

Turning briefly to sombre matters, I'm more than a bit worried about some of my mates at the moment. Each is facing serious health problems and my heart goes out to them and their loved ones.

I won't say who they are or what's wrong with them – that's their business and their news to impart. I just wish to record my sympathy and support.

I also feel for my friend Ben Avill, who's mourning the death of his dad. Bad news is deeply unsettling at any time, but especially in the run-up to Christmas.

November 29 – Remembering George Harrison, who passed to the next level 12 years ago today.

Officially, he died of throat cancer, but in truth he was never the same man after fighting off an intruder who broke into his Henley mansion home shortly after he had been diagnosed as having the fatal ailment.

George, born on February 25 like me, always was the Beatle I most identified with. His brilliance as a composer and musician is often criminally overlooked in the stampede to shower much-deserved praise on Lennon and McCartney.

Today was also the day I saw Carol, David and Suzette face to face for the first time since before my birthday earlier this year. It was so good to catch up with them, share news, exchange Christmas gifts and cards and have a meal at a local Toby Carvery.

December 1 – It's World Aids Day, an occasion to remember that this deadly disease is still very much with us, even though it's not publicised anything like as much as in bygone times.

But it's not the only killer in our midst. Freak accidents can also claim lives, as in Scotland on Friday night when a police helicopter crashed through the roof of a Glasgow pub, killing eight people and leaving 14 seriously injured.

It's hard to imagine – you're having a pleasant evening, drinking with mates in your local, and it's so savagely cut short in a blood soaked frenzy of death and destruction.

Jeez! What can you say? Sympathetic words are so woefully inadequate.

Me? – I lit a candle for the victims – my usual response to such terrible events.

The tragedy was brought home to me acutely yesterday evening (Saturday), when I popped into the Bell (Seabourne's) for a pint or three. It was quite busy and a similarly bizarre incident would have had comparably gruesome consequences.

But, unlike those unfortunate Glaswegians, I had a good time in the company of several mates - John Gaynor, Clare Hayes, Kelly Millen, Chappie and Jim (don't know their surnames), Lee Robertson, Matt Brandt, Ben Avill and Billy Clarkson.

December 3 – This morning's telly news revealed the discovery of a ninth body in the wreckage of the Scottish pub, where revellers had been enjoying a ska band just before disaster struck.

December 5 – Cards posted, check. Decorations and lights up, check. Little tree in place, check. I'm a Celebrity reaching its climax on TV, check. Yep, it's that time of year again.

And we ask ourselves the usual question – are we going to have a white Christmas? Probably not, but the weather is a talking point at the moment because gales ravaged parts of Britain last night, causing widespread damage and cutting off power to tens of thousands of homes.

Meanwhile, Obnoxious Osborne seems hell-bent on continuing his mad crusade to put the wind up as many people as possible.

He's on telly as I speak giving a budget statement in which he's announcing another rise in the retirement age - to 68.

Is he deliberately trying to alienate the entire nation?

So, Georgie boy, you're going to force even more people to hang around workplaces when they've already served this country for decades and have earned the right to retire and take it easy? How callous and disrespectful!

Apart from being cruel, this is totally nuts when you consider that the ageing process will have taken its toll so they won't be as fit or healthy as younger folk who could and should be taking over these jobs, bringing boss-pleasing energy and enthusiasm!

And what about the millions over 50 who can't get work because of their age, poor work records or ill health, forced to claim benefits for longer and insanely expected to apply for dwindling job vacancies that the younger, fitter citizens should be filling?

That's right George – make them bear the indignity of being bullied and patronised by job centre staff younger than them with fewer years' service to the nation! Brilliant!

I count myself lucky that, at the age of 59 – nearly 60 – I will still qualify for the state pension at 65 under the old rules. But I really feel for those a bit younger than me who will be caught up in this madness.

We already have a higher retirement age than most of our European neighbours. I say lower it, for that would create more opportunities for the young while showing older workers the respect they deserve instead of either telling them to struggle on in harness or badgering them to chase jobs they're not going to get anyway.

Of course, people over any retirement age should be encouraged to carry on working if they're fit enough and willing. To stop them would be grossly unfair and ageist.

What I'm saying is it should be their decision and they certainly shouldn't be forced by a vindictive and arbitrary government edict to either keep jobs when their health and energy levels are on the wane, or try to find work with slim chances of success.

Oh, and make the state pension – and benefits - a realistic reflection of people's living expenses, not the pittances recipients have been expected to live on up to now.

In other words, look after flesh and blood human beings and stop spending huge fortunes on objects such as missiles, costly hardware, vehicles, transport networks, buildings, office furniture, gadgets, gizmos, bricks, concrete, metal and so on.

But Obnoxious isn't only bashing the old – he's going after youngsters, too, with renewed threats to axe their benefits if they don't obey a set of stringent rules.

This seems unduly harsh, but might have a degree of success if only the jobs were there. Of course, they're not, despite Osborne and Cameron's outrageous claims to the contrary.

And that's due largely to their savage, unnecessary austerity measures!

On the road to recovery? They're having a laugh! – Except that it's not funny at all.

Turning to I'm a Celebrity, Get Me Out of Here, it's been the usual fare of bugs and bitching in the Australian jungle.

Participants this year have included snooker legend Steve Davis, swimming gold medallist Rebecca Adlington, Emmerdale's Lucy Pargeter, Royal fashion designer David Emanuel, EastEnders' Leila Morse and reality TV star Joey Essex.

I usually hate reality TV – Big Brother, The Only Way is Essex, the X Factor et al – but this one's different. The facts that it's in the jungle, so tougher for contestants, and I've actually heard of some of those taking part help make it riveting telly for me.

Ant and Dec's show on ITV One is good, but I prefer the ITV Two programme that follows it, featuring former "king of the jungle" Joe Swash, Laura Whitmore and celebrity guests.

December 6 – Yesterday saw the passing of a global icon – Nelson Mandela. The inspirational champion of racial equality died aged 95 at home in his native South Africa.

In truth, it was no surprise as he'd been very ill for a while. But it's still a massive blow to the whole world.

Mandela was a wise, brave and compassionate man who stood for justice and peace and went to prison for his beliefs.

He was a shining example to those craving harmony instead of hatred.

As a fiery young lawyer, he fought South Africa's savage apartheid system under which the white minority ruled and millions of blacks suffered discrimination, oppression, violence and contempt.

He was jailed by the authorities there in 1962 after a tip-off from the CIA. He was seen as a dangerous subversive, a terrorist with Communist tendencies determined to overthrow the government.

But the staunch Methodist Christian was finally released 27 years later after a worldwide campaign so massive South Africa's rulers could no longer resist it.

In 1994 he became his country's first black president – a position he held for five years. He was a statesman, philosopher and philanthropist of the highest order.

The Queen, Barack Obama and other world leaders have been among those paying glowing tributes to the great man.

Civil rights activists all over the globe aspire to his ideals for a fairer, kinder world. Farewell Mandela, you total legend for all the right reasons!

Meanwhile, at home, more severe weather has taken its toll with mass flooding in some coastal areas.

December 7 – During a conversation about Nelson Mandela yesterday, a friend asked me why people seem to have forgotten that when younger he was regarded as a terrorist and his name was associated with bombing campaigns.

My reply was that one man's terrorist is another's freedom fighter and generally he did do a lot of good in promoting peace and harmony.

Yeah, I know – a bit trite and insipid, but I was taken by surprise and didn't have a chance to formulate a properly thought-out answer.

In fact, my friend had a very good point. The details seem to be glossed over these days but it's true that while a passionate young activist Mandela's name was linked with certain organisations involved in guerrilla tactics and violent protest.

Causing injury and death in political struggles is wrong – no question – and as a peace-loving pacifist I detest violence full stop. But I would also argue that if you address someone's grievance, you remove the reason for their terrorist actions.

Talking about issues and negotiating peaceful solutions is a hell of a lot more desirable than drawing battle lines and fighting, which only makes things worse.

And in Mandela's case, I would assert that he may well have been an angry rebel with dodgy connections to start with, but his heart was in the right place and as he grew older in jail he turned into a man of peace advocating tolerance and respect.

He transformed the lives of millions of black people in his country and became an international force for good – a blazing beacon of equality, justice and wisdom. So, on balance, his contribution to the world was extremely positive and beneficial.

Now why didn't I think of saying all that yesterday? My excuse is that I wasn't prepared for the question and had no time to articulate my opinions properly before we turned to the next subject of discussion.

We can all be wise after the event. How often do we say in retrospect "Gosh I wish I'd thought of saying that at the time?"

That's the great beauty of writing things down – it gives you that opportunity to think things through and present you thoughts a lot more logically and coherently.

December 7, later – I've just had a lovely afternoon. Phil and Emily brought baby Chloe to see me. I know I'm biased, but she is adorable! Here sits a granddad grinning like a Cheshire cat. Touching base with family is so cool, don't you find?

****

CHAPTER SIX – PERCEPTIONS

December 8 – Another sad anniversary, this time of John Lennon's passing, gunned down on a New York sidewalk 33 years ago today. Thirty three years? – Ye gods, how time flies!

Wise Lennon came out with so many great quotes, both in lyric form and conversation. Here's one of my favourites:

"If someone thinks that love and peace is a cliché that must have been left behind in the sixties, that's his problem. Love and peace are eternal."

Amen to that brother! That's exactly how I feel.

December 9 – Kian Egan, former member of boy band Westlife, is the new "king of the jungle" after winning I'm a Celebrity Get Me Out of Here yesterday. David Emanuel came second and Lucy Pargeter, third.

I'm so pleased Kian won as he seems to be a thoroughly decent bloke, adored by campmates and the public alike. But I wouldn't have minded if David or Lucy had won either.

But I found it intriguing how the campmates spoke so warmly about each other on emerging from the jungle when a lot of Ant and Dec's ITV One show had been taken up with film clips of them bitching and arguing.

For example, they all praised the work ethic, thoughtfulness, team spirit and good humour of Lucy Pargeter, who came across as quite miserable, hard-faced and spiky from what we were shown in brief film clips on the prime time TV programme.

This is one reason I prefer the later ITV Two show, that broadcasts otherwise unseen footage giving a more balanced view of the fun and camaraderie in camp.

Lucy herself was shocked on seeing the way she had been presented on ITV One and put it down to mischievous editing. Others were similarly perturbed at their portrayal, notably chat show host Matthew Wright and beauty queen Amy Willerton.

All this raises a serious question. If a harmless TV programme can be edited in such a way as to twist our perception of reality so badly, just what sort of hatchet jobs are being done on a daily basis in the media covering serious, important matters?

How sure can we be that we're being given anything resembling the truth? Hmm.

December 10 - We've all done stuff we ain't proud of, so we shouldn't be too quick to judge others.

I find it fascinating to note how our perceptions can change as we learn or think more about our world and the people in it.

While pondering these ideas, I'm listening to a new CD, bought yesterday, called The Nation's Favourite Elvis Songs. It's based on a recent TV viewers' poll and features Presley's biggest hits from throughout his illustrious career.

This guy was the ultimate rock icon, the first and original, a tremendous performer who could take someone else's song and make it totally his own. And he co-wrote the classics Love Me Tender, All Shook Up, Don't Be Cruel and Heartbreak Hotel.

I also bought a triple-CD set called Ministry of Sound Anthems - Trance, containing a wealth of dance floor gems by the likes of Faithless, Robert Miles, David Guetta, Delerium, Tiesto, Armin van Buuren, Sash, Darude, Chicane, Eric Prydz, PPK, Avicii, Paul van Dyk, Swedish House Mafia and Zombie Nation.

It's a great compilation and the sleeve notes proclaim "Trance is about love, trance is about togetherness, trance is about community." Cool!

December 15 – Yesterday I went to Sam and Carl's to say farewell and good luck to Sam's son Alex, who's moving to Oxfordshire today after accepting a chef's job in Chipping Norton, which he starts tomorrow.

Jem, my great mate and Sam's ex partner, also turned up to say goodbye and he brought along a lovely lady called Sharon, who I hadn't seen for ages.

Readers of my previous books might remember me mentioning Sharon, who not only tracked me down to visit me in hospital but also came to my flat to see me just after I came home.

This blew me away because, although a very kind and considerate person, she's not a particularly close friend but really made the effort – twice!

✳✳

I've been thinking some more about the government's ridiculous decision to raise the retirement age – again. The more I consider it, the crazier it gets.

We're bombarded and brainwashed daily about eating the right foods, exercising, watching our alcohol and fat intakes and generally living healthier lifestyles.

Advances in medicine and surgery have saved and prolonged lives – mine included. Suicide is frowned upon and it's against the law to help someone pass away who desperately wants to end their pain and suffering but is too frail to do it on their own.

This alone is extreme cruelty and a violation of human rights.

There's a national obsession with looking good, keeping fit and staying alive. Yet when we have the temerity to actually succeed, the politicians complain that there are too many of us getting pensions, draining benefit funds and burdening health services.

They treat us with disdain just for taking good advice.
May I remind these heartless overlords that we are their citizens and taking care of us should be their prime objective?

Isn't that what they are there for? Or perhaps they'd like to enforce a wholesale cull of the over-60s to save cash – OUR cash that they're entrusted to spend for us!

No, perhaps not, that's a bit too controversial. They'd never get away with it. But I do wonder if that thought hasn't already crossed at least one sick mind in Whitehall.

Who the hell do these callous clowns think they are? – penalising people for living longer?

And is this any reason to make them work even more years on top of the decades they have already served our nation?

Or struggle on receiving paltry welfare payments while being treated with total contempt?

This is a kick in the head for older people. And those just starting their working lives will be horrified at facing such a long and growing period of servitude to the system.

In France they'd be out in the streets by now in a massive display of disgust. Just saying, like.

December 16 – It's been a bad old year for legends biting the dust. The latest is Hollywood actor Peter O'Toole, who passed away yesterday at the age of 81.

The Irish-born star shot to fame in 1962 when cast in the lead role in the classic Oscar-winning epic Lawrence of Arabia. Over a long and glittering career, he played in everything from Shakespeare to 1972's shocking black comedy The Ruling Class.

Nominated eight times, he never actually won an Oscar himself until being awarded an honorary one in 2003 in recognition of his outstanding contribution to the movies.

Starting on stage, he graduated to TV before launching his illustrious film career.

But he was almost as famous for his hard-drinking, hell-raising activities as anything he achieved on stage or screen.

He was a fine actor, a real character, and will be greatly missed.

And it's just been announced that Oscar-winning actress Joan Fontaine also died yesterday aged 96.

One of the last survivors from Hollywood's "golden age", her numerous films included Jane Eyre, The Witches and the Hitchcock classics Rebecca and Suspicion.

December 17 – It's recently occurred to me that my writings have got a lot more political in the past three years or so. This is more by accident than intention.

There's always been an element of political comment right from the start, 18 years and several books ago, and it's been a recurring theme in my lyrics going back even further, to the 1970s.

But it's become a much more prominent feature in my prose ramblings since 2010 when this dreadful coalition government attained power by default, then proceeded to wage a bitter war on its own people that it's continuing and intensifying.

It's particularly infuriating when the hard-hearted pillocks in charge try to justify their savage and divisive policies by claiming they're acting in our interests. Oh please!

They insist on talking down to us like we're naughty children, and persist in portraying themselves in the role of caring parents forced unwillingly to exercise tough love in order to save us from disaster.

This means slamming the brakes on runaway spending as a matter of urgency or we'll end up penniless and in the gutter, they claim.

Well, if they must use such clumsy, crass and absurd analogies in addressing complex situations, here's my response.

I detest your unfair decision to with-hold pocket money from some of your kids when others have so blatantly raided the family coffers and continue to live in clover.

And I'm disgusted that you pretend your plan is working when it patently isn't.

I accept that all parents tell little white lies sometimes to protect their young. But they shouldn't use deception to cover up their own inefficiency and greed.

Neither should they punish some children while favouring others far guiltier of misdemeanours – partly because they themselves are benefiting from the wrongdoing!

To carry the analogy even further, these particular parents are displaying serious levels of collusion, incompetence and neglect.

I'm not a politician or a political thinker – I don't pretend to be. I have no wish to enter that murky world and besides, someone more adept in analysing and debating such matters would no doubt be able to rip my half-baked theories to shreds.

But I do reserve the right to use my writing abilities to comment on current affairs and the words and actions of our political leaders when I feel moved to do so.

I have a very keen perception of what's right and wrong, acceptable and unacceptable. And cruel and unjust policies make my blood boil – hence all the heated rhetoric.

My recent decision to join the Green Party was a clear statement of my strong desire to see a fairer, kinder, more environmentally-aware world – not a sign that I want to start attending meetings or marches, join committees or stand for election.

Political matters have featured heavily in my life journal of late but I've written a lot more about all sorts of stuff in recent years as more has happened to me, I've found more to comment on in the world around me, and much more time to do it in, thanks to a quieter lifestyle.

At the same time I've felt newly energised and inspired, with a fresh urgency to present my story and thoughts in both prose and lyric form.

Reading back what I've written, I do seem to have vent my spleen with repetitive regularity. I apologise for this, but I feel it shows how passionately I feel when I see cruelty, injustice and overt displays of spite, bigotry and hatred.

And I can't promise to stop giving my opinion any time soon if such disgraceful behaviour continues, as it no doubt will. No matter how hard I try, I just can't. I hope you understand.

December 18 – Yet another high-profile death has hit the headlines. Ronnie Biggs has popped his clogs at the age of 84.

He is by far the most famous of the gang of criminals who committed the world-famous Great Train Robbery in August

1963, escaping with £2.6 million from the Glasgow to London mail train. (That's over £41 million in today's money).

He was sentenced to 30 years in jail but broke out of Wandsworth prison in 1965 to go on the run, living in Australia, Spain and Brazil while evading capture for decades.

With failing health, he returned to Britain in 2001 seeking medical help but was put back behind bars. He served another eight years before being released on compassionate grounds after contracting pneumonia. He died in London last night.

Biggs actually only played a relatively small part in a major event dubbed "the crime of the century" - but later became something of a folk hero as he wrote a book, courted celebrity, repeatedly thumbed his nose at the authorities and even had a hit record with the Sex Pistols. He died unrepentant.

The timing of his demise is strangely apt bearing in mind that ITV One starts a two-part drama about the Great Train Robbery tonight, with the second part tomorrow.

A similar thing's happening with Mandela – his death has come just weeks before release of a movie about his life.

But one old feller still with us is Rolling Stone Keith Richards, 70 today. Happy birthday sunshine – and thanks for all the brilliant music.

I also wish to extend birthday greetings to my friend and former work colleague Sue Bolton and little Leon, my mate Kerry's son, who's eight.

Other items in today's national news include an announcement that unemployment in the UK has fallen again and now stands at 2.4 million, its lowest level since 2009. The government will claim this shows its policies are working and Britain is starting to bounce back.

But I'm deeply sceptical and wonder how much the facts have been distorted and figures massaged. I can't see how on Earth the statement can be true, given the massive number of jobs lost thanks to coalition cutbacks.

And even if the claim is right, I wonder at what cost in human suffering. How many are reluctantly stuck in part-time work (therefore still needing state help) because they can't secure full-time employment?

How many are on useless training schemes, so temporarily not counted as jobless, or labouring in unpaid positions, or on zero hours contracts?

And how many are feeling forced to hit the plastic to pay the bills, using credit cards and piling up debt they have no chance of ever repaying while putting their homes and families at risk, causing great stress and bitter acrimony?

I suspect that the total number of people actually in full-time, paid work is comparatively speaking much smaller than in previous years, and it's also a hell of a lot less than the government statisticians are strongly implying.

And I repeat the question – what is the cost of this alleged success? A broken, divided nation, where far too many are struggling and suffering, morale is rock bottom and people are dispirited, anxious and fractious. Some success story!

December 19 – Watching that uncannily topical Great Train Robbery programme on TV last night set me thinking.

More than once it was suggested that the gang members saw themselves as rebels striking a blow for the ordinary man against a corrupt, unfair system where some enjoyed great wealth and privilege while others struggled to survive.

But let's not dress it up too much – these men were not 20th-century Robin Hoods. They were robbing thugs, driven by pure greed - hardened, violent criminals not averse to using fists or coshes to get what they wanted.

There was no higher purpose to their actions and the only political aspect was provided after the event by an establishment rocked by the scale and audacity of their crime and still reeling from the recent Profumo affair scandal.

Eager to re-assert its authority and send out a clear message that people should know their place, it decided to make an example of these bold upstarts by dishing out jail sentences far in excess of what would normally have been the case for armed robbery.

The pure impudence of the train raid and the huge amount of cash stolen, added to the fact that it came so soon after Profumo, no doubt strengthened the resolve of the forces of law and order to fight back hard.

Having said all that, the TV drama was good viewing and I look forward to part two tonight.

Today's news was dominated by stories of celebrities in court accused of drug offences, the trial of two men charged with killing Army drummer Lee Rigby in London in May, and the sad revelation that a body found at Didcot, Oxfordshire, was that of 17-year-old Jayden Parkinson, missing since December 3.

This is heartbreaking and we all feel for her devastated family, especially as Christmas is less than a week away. A former boyfriend has appeared in court charged with her murder.

Meanwhile, in Bournemouth, a guy stands accused of murdering a 16-year-old girl. Shit, man!

December 20 – More than 70 people were injured, seven seriously, when a ceiling collapsed in a London theatre during performance of a play last night.

An investigation has been launched into what exactly happened and why.

Also on today's news, questions of a different kind are being asked as to what radicalised the two Muslim extremists who butchered Fusilier Lee Rigby to death in broad daylight on a London street in May.

I welcome this, because finding out why people commit atrocities – what drives them to feel so passionately about an ideology to kill for it – is the key to addressing grievances, finding solutions to problems and removing any possible causes for violent terrorist actions.

Hold it right there; I'm in no way condoning or excusing such abominable crimes. These people are mentally disturbed with a very sick and twisted view of what's right and wrong. But shouldn't we be asking that million dollar question – why?

Blind condemnation only aggravates friction and deepens division. Only when we start probing people's views and motivations can we begin to understand and get to the root of their anger and hatred, therefore deal with it and move forward to a more peaceful future.

There will always be those unhinged psychopaths with no agendas at all who are just insane individuals bent on violence and killing. We can't do a lot in their case except take them out of circulation and give them deep counselling to neutralise them.

I suppose a similar approach could work with murderous zealots, but we would still need to ascertain the warped mindset that led to their actions if we're going to sort out the problems and make any progress.

Another news item informed us of a proposal to ban the broadcasting of payday loan adverts in breaks between children's TV programmes. What?

I'm not keen on bans – with certain exceptions - but I can see the logic of outlawing such commercials altogether, as they do persuade certain individuals to take out high-interest loans and get themselves in serious financial trouble. But children?

I can't see much point in putting these adverts on kids' TV anyway, as youngsters are hardly likely to be the slightest bit interested in a boring commercial about money.

But chocolate biscuits? – Now that's a totally different matter. I know I've used this example before, but I feel it's so very appropriate to revive it now.

A few years ago, a TV advert for these delicious items suggested it was okay to be dishonest, deceptive, greedy and selfish in your attempt to obtain and enjoy them.

This worried me, as it was being shown on daytime telly when children would have been watching. It seemed to encapsulate a growing trend in commercials condoning – promoting, even – bad behaviour in the pursuit of material gain.

I said then, and I repeat now, that it's a crazy old world when people get all het up and demand blanket bans on certain types of TV broadcasting while no-one appears to care if kids' ideas of morality are seriously corrupted by an advert for choccy biccies.

Seems to me the reality we're asked to accept and live in gets madder by the day. It gives comedy kings like Seth MacFarlane (Family Guy, American Dad), the Monty Python team, Richard Curtis, Russell Howard, Eddie Izzard and Michael McIntyre so much great material to work with.

They, and we, are swamped by illogical, insane and bizarre people, ideas and situations at all times.

Okay, they each possess the imagination; ingenuity and great skill to reflect these absurdities back to us in a way that makes us laugh out loud, but what a welter of solid gold stupidity they have to draw from!

December 21 – Happy Yuletide folks. It's the shortest day of the year and the Winter Solstice, a time for us Brits to celebrate.

For let's not forget, we were toasting seasonal changes, ancient festivals and pagan gods long before Christianity was brought to our fair land.

It's also the time we ponder the ups and downs of the past 12 months. For some, it's been a dreadful year scarred by tragedy and sadness, for others, a happy one full of joy and achievement.

On balance, I've found 2013 to be very pleasant indeed. I watched my son marry his childhood sweetheart, became a granddad again and realised a long-held dream of being a published author.

It thrills me to have finally found my true station in life, my destiny, my purpose – in career terms at least. But it's a triumph with its roots in sadness, bearing in mind the heartbreaking circumstances that provided the money for me to do it (Jan's passing).

I've had a couple of nice meals with Carol, David and Suzette and some lovely times with Phil, Emily, the grandkids and my new extended family.

Other highlights included five excellent rock gigs, Boscombe Community Fair, my Weymouth holiday with Sam, Carl and family and some great booze and nonsense sessions round their house with a variety of mutual pals.

During those sessions, including sunny summertime barbeques, I made some new friends including Cass Kelly and Sonia Jamieson.

There was that rainy but enjoyable day out in Poole with Steve Yarwood, I spent some very pleasant hours with my buddy Jem Hannen, and savoured a few good pub sessions with mates including John Gaynor, John Palmer, Ben Avill, Matt Brandt, Lee Robertson, Victoria Brown, Billy Clarkson, and the two Kellys (Adams and Millen).

Plus I've had a lot of fun on Facebook and used it to restore contact with my great pal Carole Jones many years after losing touch – a terrific result!

Yep, it's been a good year for me. But not for others. I continue to worry about friends' health and I feel for those who have lost loved ones in battle, terrorist attacks, severe storms, terrible accidents or to illness.

Let's hope 2014 is going to be better for them and good for us all.

December 21, evening time – About an hour ago, I got back from a very pleasant afternoon at Boscombe Conservative Club in the company of my friend Lea, who I used to work with while volunteering in Southbourne's Red Cross charity shop.

Lea's a member at the club, and just before Christmas every year we meet up there for a chat and a few alcoholic beverages. Sweet!

On the way home, I popped into my local chippy to get a take-away and saw a newspaper headline about TV chef Nigella Lawson.

She was complaining bitterly about her "malicious" treatment in a very recent court case, during which it had been claimed she habitually snorted cocaine.

Nigella pointed out, quite rightly, that it wasn't her on trial - she was a witness, not a defendant, and had not been charged with any crime.

In fact, even the two people in the dock, ex-employees of hers, were cleared of the fraud allegations against them.

I can understand her anger and indignation. If you want to prosecute a celebrity – or anyone else for that matter – just do it if you feel you have enough evidence against them.

Don't call them as a witness and then allow them to be pilloried as if they're the accused. The judge should have stepped in to halt this travesty of so-called justice.

December 22 - Getting home yesterday evening I found the road outside blocked off and lots of activity involving fire fighters, police and their vehicles. There had been a blaze in the unoccupied house next door but it had been put out by the time I arrived.

Gordon Bennett - Talk about too close for comfort!

I was relieved to be allowed into my home and I'm thanking my lucky stars our property – a house converted to flats – was unaffected. Fortunately, no-one was in the next door building at the time of the incident.

Police and fire service personnel were back on the scene this morning investigating the cause. The house, recently sold, is structurally still intact but the windows were blown out and the inside looks badly burnt and a right mess. It stinks of smoke.

December 22, early evening – I've just watched a fascinating but very disturbing Channel Five documentary on catch-up TV called Nazi Quest for the Holy Grail.

It told how Hitler's mentally twisted Third Reich sadists, notably Heinrich Himmler, believed they were descendants of a fragmented ancient Aryan master race with a divine right to rule the world.

They thought their bloodline was the purest on Earth and all others should be subservient to them. And Nazi scientists went all over the place searching for evidence of their precious lost civilisation.

It was said to have originated on the island of Atlantis, positioned between Europe and North America before sinking in pre-historic times.

The medieval German legend of Parzival and his quest for the Holy Grail was also mixed in with this strange mythical concoction as the Nazis tried to establish a new religion – or, in their eyes, revive an old one.

They hated Christianity, seeing it as promoting weakness, and wanted to restore the old pagan sun gods to prominence along with their solstices and festivals.

They despised the Jesus religion's Jewish roots and used scientific instruments in measuring citizens' skull and skeletal bones to judge whether they were racially pure enough to be accepted into the top level of their vicious new-style caste system.

And this is where it started getting dark and evil, for those that failed to pass the tests were exterminated in a notoriously severe and widespread ethnic cleansing process – the sinister and grisly Final Solution.

The theory was that the survivors of the Atlantis disaster fled to other parts of the globe, setting up new civilisations in places like Egypt and Tibet and interbreeding with other races, diluting and corrupting the purity of the bloodline.

This needed urgent reversal if the bloodline was to be restored, they asserted. The terrifying end results of this warped elitist mindset were the death camps like Auschwitz and the extermination of six million Jews.

The bitter irony here is that Judaism is a religion, not a race, a fact conveniently and devastatingly overlooked by the sick minds ordering and executing the slaughter.

Readers of my earlier writings will know that I have my own Atlantis theory which follows a parallel line of thinking but without the savagely divisive and potentially lethal aspects that I find ignorant, illogical and despicable.

In my version, the survivors of the lost civilisation spread over the Earth to show us the way to truth and light – in other words, how to avoid the pitfalls that destroyed their idyllic Eden and instead strive towards a future where peace and harmony reign.

As always, there would have been some bad apples – those using divine wisdom, enlightened knowledge and both practical and magical powers to devilish ends. It could have been these dangerously deluded individuals that inspired the Nazi dream.

It freezes my blood to hear friends slating those of different racial origins, religions or cultures, recklessly tarring them all with the same brush as unwanted troublemakers – because I look at Hitler and his cronies and see this highly corrosive mindset taken to its natural, devastating conclusion.

For goodness' sake, some people are violent thugs, devious liars, perverted control freaks or self-obsessed, habitual criminals. Others are not. And that has absolutely nothing to do with races or cultures. Nice and nasty people can be found in them all.

To think otherwise and use generalisations based on cultural or racial distinctions is very dangerous indeed because it gives extremist bigoted psychos the licence to indulge in sick and evil hate campaigns with disastrously destructive consequences.

This is why I despise racism and all other kinds of discrimination – cultural, religious, sexual, whichever. It's also why I get so angry when I hear sweeping statements reeking of blind prejudice and see the resultant intolerance, hatred and persecution.

December 24 – Christmas Eve – and I'm wishing a very happy birthday to my great friend Carole Jones, born on this day. I sent her a Facebook message to that effect earlier, adding my hopes for a great Christmas for her and her loved ones.

Fire fighters are set to go on strike from 7pm this evening to midnight in a dispute over pensions. Good grief – I can't help wondering what might have happened if it had been Saturday evening when the house next door caught alight.

Would I have still been here writing this or would my home of 30 years gone up in smoke, too? Sends a shiver down the spine – and I really feel for anyone unlucky enough to need the fire service this evening, especially as its Christmas and the weather's been very stormy with gale force winds set to continue.

I happen to think that fire fighters shouldn't have to go on strike. They should be well enough paid and treated to make it unnecessary.

Let's face it; they do a very risky job, sometimes putting their own lives on the line. They don't do it for the money, but to help people. Like nurses, coppers and armed services folk, they are in a special category of workers we desperately need and would be lost without. They should all be flipping well treasured and given the respect, salaries, working conditions, after care and retirement packages they richly deserve.

December 24, later – I've just had a lovely visit from Phil, Emily, Chloe and Harvey, involving the giving and receiving of festive gifts and cards. Fantastic! Happy Christmas guys, love you lots, and, of course, Lucas, who couldn't come.

I'm now about to sit down and watch Walt Disney's film Fantasia on telly. Made in 1940, it's a timeless classic – the best movie he ever made and one that's appealed to people of all ages across seven decades.

I fell in love with it as a kid and it remains my all-time favourite film, a spellbinding work of genius blending classical music with brilliant multi-coloured animation in a way that's just magical.

December 25 - Merry Christmas all! Last night I went to The Bell (yes, apparently we are allowed to call it that again as it's just changed hands) and had a drink or three with John Gaynor, Ben Avill, Matt Brandt and his lady Dani, Bev Jones, John Palmer, "Squeak" Turnbull, Sam Rose Lowney, Vicky and Mark, and Chappie.

Mark, the new man in charge, seems to be a good bloke, as does his son, Callum. Mark's lady, Laura, also appears to be nice.

When I went to the pub yesterday lunchtime to pick up my ticket for the evening party, I met my mates Rod, Rich, Jem and Ian and had a drink with them, which was good.

Today, I'm off to have a festive dinner round Sam and Carl's. A bit earlier I received Happy Christmas texts from Carol and Phil, which I replied to with glee, and I've just phoned my Auntie Joyce with seasonal greetings.

Family – that's what it's all about really, isn't it? I really feel for those who have recently lost loved ones or who sadly have no-one to spend the day with.

And I say hats off to the kind people who willingly put their own celebrations on hold to make sure others are okay – manning soup kitchens or looking after the elderly or homeless, things like that.

I think we should also spare a thought for military men and women posted abroad, away from loved ones, and all those working in the various service industries, ensuring our festive holidays run as smoothly as possible.

It's the time of year we become acutely aware that, disgracefully, even in 21st century England, we still have homeless people and those living in poverty, squalor and isolation. In other lands it's even worse.

What a damning indictment of the world we live in and those that run it!

December 25 – several hours later – I've recently returned home from spending most of Christmas Day with Sam, Carl, the boys and Rebecca. Thanks so very much guys, for the hospitality, company and excellent festive meal.

December 27 – Happy Birthday Dad. Always loved, never forgotten. RIP wonderful man, I've lit a candle for you.

It's a vanilla-scented one that Sam and Carl gave me for Christmas. They also presented me with a handy plastic beer glass that telescopes flat to fit in your pocket, some Belgian chocolates, a 2014 diary and a Christmas tree brooch with flashing lights. What cool Yule gifts!

Phil, Emily and the grandchildren gave me a great hand-drawn picture of the Beatles and some lovely family photos.

Carol and David gave me a set of "keep calm" drinks mugs, Richard, Ruth and their boys some chocolates, Scott, Jane and family a W H Smith's token, Suzette got me a tin of biscuits and a book about Bournemouth's history with photos, and Joyce slipped some money in a Christmas card as usual.

Some really good prezzies there – didn't I do well?

Actually, I've had a very enjoyable festive season so far, with Phil and Emily bringing the kids on Christmas Eve, my two visits to the pub that day, my Christmas Day meal and drinks with Sam and family, and Boxing Day back there for a buffet party also attended by our friend Tina Mcauley, who gave me a scarf, socks and shower gel.

But poor little Chloe didn't do so well, bless her. She developed a nasty chest infection so she, Phil and Em spent most of Boxing Day at Poole Hospital. They're back home now, thank goodness, and Chloe's on antibiotics, but it's obviously taken the shine off their Christmas celebrations.

Sam and Carl suffered a similar blow with their little boy, Bailey, going down with a heavy cold that made him miserable, poor little mite. It's always sad when people are ill at Christmas, especially children. Hope Bailey and Chloe get better real soon.

December 30 – Well, as usual, we've had a liberal dose of old Carry On movies on telly over Christmas. I do love these classics of British comedy!

The very first, Carry on Sergeant, was a black and white film starring William Hartnell, Bob Monkhouse and Kenneth Connor, released way back in 1958.

They were then churned out like sausages every year up to Carry on Emmanuelle in 1978. A 14-year gap followed before the format was revived one last time for Carry on Columbus in 1992.

Many great comedy actors have starred in them over the decades, but it's generally accepted that the golden age was the 1960s and early seventies with Sid James, Barbara Windsor and Kenneth Williams.

After that they seemed to run out of ideas and the scripts went for nudity and crudity rather than the clever wordplay, brilliant satire and saucy humour of the earlier ones.

Although I'm a big fan of these films, they do make me wince at times because they reflect old opinions and mindsets seen as perfectly acceptable at the time but seriously dodgy in retrospect.

They represent a sexually repressed and quite prejudiced British way of looking at life using an old mindset employed by millions struggling to cope with the explosion of new ideas and liberal attitudes that rocked the nation in those key decades.

Take Carry on Camping, for example – which was on TV the other day. Released in 1969, it's regarded as one of the best, and is certainly among of my favourites. But it's let down by a weak ending that really highlights this seismic clash of cultures in a truly embarrassing way.

A bunch of hippies turn up in a field next door to the Carry on team's camp site and launch into an all-night rave with loud music, beads, bells, fur coats and all the familiar clichés.

The flower power crowd are portrayed as sex-mad, dirty, smelly undesirables lacking any kind of moral compass – a view so typical of a confused and panicked establishment at the time.

In Carry on at your Convenience, also on TV over Christmas, Kenneth Cope is a lazy, trouble-making union shop steward using any excuse to call his comrades out on strike so he doesn't have to work himself.

Sexist, racist, ageist and other quite bigoted views pepper the script and visual jokes of all the Carry On films.

And this is where the new generation – of David Frost, Pete and Dud and Monty Python – stepped in with their fearless and refreshing new slant on comedy and satire that was so very much more in tune with changing times and attitudes, showing just how old school and out-of-touch the Carry On makers were.

But I still enjoy watching the old movies with their double entendres, saucy scripts, funny storylines and slapstick humour because they remind me of bygone times that were so much part of my growing up.

Yes, it's true – nostalgia ain't what it used to be!

Turning to more serious matters, Islamist extremists have been blamed for two suicide bomb attacks killing dozens in Volgograd, Russia in the past two days.

Its feared militant groups are ramping up the violence in the run-up to the 2014 Winter Olympics due to start in that country soon.

Legendary racing driver Michael Schumacher is fighting for his life in hospital after a skiing accident in the French Alps yesterday. The seven times Formula One championships winner, who retired from the circuit last year, suffered severe head injuries in the fall. He's had an operation and is in a coma.

December 31 – Schumie's still critically ill and remains in a coma, but there's been a slight improvement. We wish him and his loved ones all the best. Meanwhile, New Zealand has already celebrated the arrival of 2014 and actress Penelope Keith, star of The Good Life and To the Manor Born, has been made a Dame.

These were two great TV sitcoms, as were Dad's Army, Are You Being Served? , 'Allo 'Allo, It Ain't Half Hot Mum and Hi De Hi – all co-written by Poole-born David Croft, who died two years ago. A tribute to him was re-shown on telly over Christmas.

Watching it again, I could see parallels with what I said earlier about the Carry On films in terms of content and criticisms. 'Allo 'Allo and It Ain't Half Hot Mum were accused of having racist tendencies and Are You Being Served? was said to be sexist.

But I've always held that tackling such thorny issues using comedy is fine - just so long as it's genuinely funny and not laced with vicious undertones.

And Croft, ably assisted by his writing partners Jimmy Perry and Jeremy Lloyd, was a master of mixing humour and pathos in brilliant scripts showing us the absurd side of serious situations in a quite wonderful way that was affectionate rather than cruel.

Dad's Army remains a timeless classic of British comedy, a masterpiece in terms of great writing and excellent performances from a truly talented cast. The same applies to the other shows, but Dad's Army was the cream of a very rich crop.

Croft, Perry and Lloyd set the benchmark for highly skilled sitcom writing, along with Clements and La Frenais (Likely Lads, Porridge, Auf Wiedersehen Pet) John Sullivan (Only Fools and Horses, Citizen Smith) and Roy Clarke (Keeping Up Appearances, Open All Hours, Last of the Summer Wine).

And, at the end of the day, if you can make people laugh at themselves, their circumstances, their fears and foibles, surely that's far better than portraying life's difficulties in a way that's bitter, cynical and ultimately depressing?

You've got to have a sense of humour and possess the ability to see the funny side of things – otherwise, I think you've missed one of the main points of being here!

January 1 – Happy New Year guys. Yep, it's 2014. And let's hope it ends up being a good one for us all.

I actually saw it in with Sam and Carl. I hadn't planned to – but I'm glad I did.

I was going to spend a while with them and their family and then pop into the pub for a couple of pints on the way home – still being back in my armchair well before midnight. That was the idea, anyway.

But it turned into a really good little party that went on considerably longer than I'd expected. Our mates Rich, Sharon and Tina also turned up and we spent several nice hours together.

As time passed, the pub visit went out of the window. I stayed on, even after the others had all left, and the nearer it got to 12, the more determined Sam, Carl and I became to make it past Big Ben's chimes. I eventually left shortly afterwards and came straight home.

It was great, but boy am I feeling rough today!

January 2 – During our many and varied conversations during that rather good New Year's Eve party, the subject turned at one point to suicide. Charming, you might say, and I agree, but it sort of happened by accident.

It all started out well enough with Rich cracking a joke, but then it got serious.

I commented that I did not share the widely-held view that killing yourself was taking the coward's way out, as I felt it took a lot of courage.

My friends all totally disagreed with me, taking the popular view about selfish cowards. I can certainly see the selfishness – the total lack of consideration for heartbroken and angry friends and relatives left behind. But cowardly? Hardly!

When push came to shove and the stark reality hit, how many of us would actually have the guts to follow it through? I know I couldn't – not that I've ever considered it (except very fleetingly).

And I think the circumstances can make a huge difference. Taking a pill overdose because you're terminally ill, close to the end anyway and in excruciating pain is one thing. But jumping in front of a train just because you're fed up is totally different.

For one thing, it shows a reckless disregard for the feelings of your loved ones, the traumatised train driver and the poor sods who have to clean up the grisly mess. It's also a criminal waste of a life.

Some people get so desperate and depressed they can't think straight. In their eyes, they're completely alone, the whole world's against them and they wouldn't be missed anyway. This is so very sad – but it's also misguided, self-indulgent twaddle.

And I say that as someone who's been just as pathetically self-indulgent at times.

Most of us have at least one person who cares about us – whether we realise it or not.

Then, of course, you get the egocentric attention seekers who merely threaten to top themselves, or bungle attempts to do so, just to get a bit of sympathy. I see this as despicable. It's the worst kind of emotional blackmail.

Those that actually do kill themselves are usually the ones that keep their mouths shut, get on with it and do the job properly – they don't talk about it or cock it up.

You're probably wondering why I'm even mentioning such a dark and depressing topic. Well, it's one of those thought association things.

There was something on the TV news this morning about January being a busy month for on-line dating sites.

We were told that lonely single people logged on in their droves just after Christmas to find love and companionship as a fresh year dawned.

This set me pondering on other press reports from the past telling us that this is also a popular time for suicides as the troubled, heavy-hearted, isolated and lonely faced another grim 12 months following the forced jollity of the festive season.

And that reminded me of the party conversation I'd forgotten about up to then.

Oh, and before you ask – no, none of this bit is about me. I'm not feeling lonely or sad and I'm quite happy with my life as it is at the moment. Just so you know!

January 4– Yet another rock icon has passed on. This time it's Phil Everly, who died yesterday aged 74.

Phil and his older brother Don, who survives him, were pioneers of modern music as we know it. And that's no exaggeration.

They were there right at the beginning, along with Elvis Presley, Buddy Holly, Chuck Berry and Roy Orbison. Their potent blend of country and rock'n'roll stands the test of time with consummate ease.

The Everly Brothers wrote brilliant songs and sang them in sweet harmony while strumming their guitars. Their influence has been immense and far reaching.

Everyone from the Beatles to Linda Ronstadt, Paul Simon to Green Day's Billy Joe Armstrong name check them as major inspirations and all-time greats.

Classics like Bye Bye Love, Cathy's Clown, Let It Be Me, Wake Up Little Suzie, the Price of Love, Walk Right Back, Claudette, All I Have To Do Is Dream and Love Hurts have become rock standards and karaoke favourites, being covered time and time again over the decades by a variety of performers.

Farewell Phil – RIP legendary man. And thanks for all the music.

January 5 – Similar praise is due to footballing wizard Eusebio, who has also passed on at the age of 71.

The Benfica striker's nine goals for Portugal at the 1966 World Cup in England included four against North Korea.

Widely considered as one of the world's best players ever, he scored 733 times in 745 professional matches. Quite an achievement!

Famed for his blistering acceleration and dazzling dribbling skills, Eusebio was named European Footballer of the Year in 1965. He won the European Cup with Benfica in 1962 and was in the side that lost to Manchester United in the 1968 final.

Bobby Charlton, who played against him in that match, and Chelsea's Portuguese manager Jose Mourinho have led the tributes to a guy who was the Cristiano Ronaldo of his day. Indeed, Ronaldo himself added his own glowing accolade.

January 6 – So it's Twelfth Night, the time by which we apparently need to have taken all our Christmas decorations down in order to avoid bad luck. (I did this on the third).

For Christians it's Epiphany – the revelation that Jesus was God's son.

And for Obnoxious Osborne, it apparently represents a perfect opportunity to twist the knife even more. Nice guy!

Yep, he was on the news again this morning, warning that another £25 billion spending cuts would be needed after the next election – half of it from the already badly battered welfare budget!

Way to go George – that's the way to cheer us up on the most miserable Monday of the year while ensuring we vote for you and your cruel cronies next time around!

But in the very same statement, he had the brass neck to claim - yet again - that things were beginning to improve and the economy was starting to recover, proving coalition policies were working.

This is not only untrue; it's also another glaring example of how this callous clown continues to shoot himself in the foot.

Because, to state the bleeding obvious, if the vicious policies were working and things were getting better, surely now would be the time to ease up and try to help rather than further bash hard-pressed citizens, winning back votes before the next election.

Nick Clegg responded to Osborne's statement with a warning of his own – not to inflict "cuts for cuts sake."

Good grief – is he finally growing a backbone? Talk about shutting the stable door after the horse has bolted. It's far too late for him to salvage his reputation and save the Lib Dems now. He should have stood up to Cameron, Osborne and crew from the start. What a twerp!

It's clear to me that the Tories' legacy is already destined to be a broken and fragmented nation, ravaged by hardship and totally lacking enthusiasm, hope, morale or confidence. More cuts are guaranteed to make it even worse.

January 9 – Wishing a very happy birthday to legendary guitarist Jimmy Page of Led Zeppelin, 70 today. Iconic rock star David Bowie was 67 yesterday. Both have been giants of popular music over the past half-century and their impact and influence can't really be over-stated.

America has been shivering in the coldest winter for 20 years – and the ice and snow are coming this way. Great!

Meanwhile, thousands of Brits are still suffering the devastation of recent storms and floods.

Extreme weather has caused misery and chaos all over the globe in recent years. Climate change? The debate rumbles on.

Feelings are running high and it's feared more tension and violence will erupt on Britain's streets following an inquest jury's decision that police acted lawfully in shooting a young father of six dead in London in 2011.

Mark Duggan, 29, was said to be riding home in a taxi in Tottenham when fatally wounded by an armed cop. Rioting ensued across the country.

Police claimed he was a dangerous man in possession of a gun – but others asserted that he had thrown the weapon from the cab window before being shot.

Mr Duggan, who grew up on the infamous Broadwater Farm estate where Pc Keith Blakelock was killed in 1985, was reputed to be a founding member of one of the area's most notorious gangs.

The nephew of gangland boss Desmond Noonan, it is alleged he was planning a major cannabis deal when shot.

His death was said to be a major factor as riots broke out in London then spread to other cities that summer.

Five people died as the violence flared in Birmingham, Bristol and Manchester as well as the capital. The cost of damage was estimated at £200 million.

Mr Duggan's family and friends have reacted with disbelief and anger at the inquest jury's verdict that his killing was justified - even if he had cast the gun aside before being shot.

Furious spectators hurled abuse at jurors and branded the police "murderers." Security guards were forced to intervene when some began kicking a door and turning over furniture in the High Court.

Protesters maintain that Mr Duggan was executed and police chiefs are poised to meet community leaders in a bid to defuse the tension and prevent even more violence.

There's a new programme on telly called Benefits Street. And it's a real eye-opener.

It's a documentary series about a residential road in Birmingham where the vast majority of people are on welfare – and some have been for ages. It's a grim, unflinching, quite shocking record of how some of our citizens without recognised jobs, hope or prospects consistently bend and break the rules - and the law - in order to survive in 21st century England.

Most have had their benefits cut and are struggling to make ends meet. They shoplift, trade in stolen goods and deal drugs in their attempts to get cash, food, clothing and other essentials. Booze and weed are prominent and prison's never far away for some.

Oh yes, we can sit in front of our TVs and tut-tut at their criminal tendencies and run-down, messy, litter-strewn neighbourhood. We can smugly judge and moralise – tell them to stop scrounging, get off their bums, find work and stop breaking the law.

After all, they're dodgy undesirables, unlawfully minted liberty-takers and all round scum of the Earth, aren't they? – Or at least that's what David Cameron, Jeremy Kyle and the Daily Mail would have us believe. But hang on a minute.

I don't think these people are in their situation through choice. And most of them desperately want to climb out of that rut and lead better lifestyles.

But it's not that easy these days – thanks to Cameron, Brown and other reckless architects of our currently insane economic set-up and deeply flawed welfare state.

And besides, something shines through all the deprivation, desperation, squalor and crime. There's warmth, kindness, humour and a real community spirit here. These are people - fellow citizens - just trying to get through the day like the rest of us.

Well, most of us anyway. There will always be those basking in the glow of great wealth and privilege, no matter how difficult life gets for others. And that's obscene.

I guess what I'm saying is don't be too hard on the residents of Benefits Street. They are not your enemies. (In fact, no-one should be).

At the end of the day, crime is crime and fraud is fraud – whether the perpetrators wear trackies or tiaras, have Cutter's Choice roll-ups or silver spoons in their gobs.

Did those at the top of the pile get there by playing by the rules? And aren't we all guilty of using fibs and underhand tactics at least sometimes to get what we want?

Anyone answering no to the second question is either dishonest, deluded or demented.

And remember, some people are so poor, all they have is money. Okay, I pinched that – it was on Facebook the other day. But I like it and decided to insert it here as it's so relevant and so true.

January 13 - Talking of Facebook, a female friend of mine shook me to the roots yesterday with something she put on the social networking site.

I don't know her all that well, but she's always struck me as a really sweet-natured, kind and thoughtful lady - a peace-loving hippie chick. So it was a big shock to read her hate-fuelled status.

It was on a subject she clearly felt very passionately about. I fully supported her grave concern but I was appalled at the savage tone she used advocating extreme violence.

It's not the first time a friend's amazed me by saying or doing something apparently so totally out of character.

I'm sure this must have happened in reverse with me saying or writing something that's taken my mates aback.

What does this prove? Well, three things I guess. One is that we can all surprise each other sometimes with our words and actions. Secondly, it shows we rarely know people as well as we think we do. And thirdly, we all have our pet hates that push our buttons and send us into a mentally unhinged blind rage.

But that's the human condition. And the sooner we all recognise this stark truth, the better it will be each and every one of us.

The fact that my friend's comments shocked me so much says more about me and my incomplete perception of her character than it does her or any flaws she might have.

We should all cut each other more slack. And, always remember - at the end of the day, we can hate someone's words and actions without hating the person. Much easier said than done sometimes, but another truth we'd do well to remember and live by.

Today's TV news told us that the biggest public inquiry into child abuse ever held in the UK has just started.

The Historical Institutional Abuse Inquiry (HIA) is examining claims of gross misconduct in Northern Ireland children's homes and borstals.

It was set up by the province's power-sharing executive to investigate allegations covering the period from 1922 to 1995. To date, 434 people have contacted the inquiry to allege they were mistreated.

The inquiry is investigating claims of physical, sexual, and emotional abuse, as well as childhood neglect.

But you can bet your bottom dollar that our messed-up media, totally and unhealthily obsessed with sex, will concentrate on that particular aspect of the issue.

Meanwhile, horrifying cases of vicious beatings, heartless control, mental and emotional devastation and criminal neglect will go largely unmentioned in the media stampede to shock us with sexually-implicit scandal.

Makes you sick really! And we're asked to rely on these warped weirdos to give us the news in a balanced, unbiased way. Fat chance!

Meanwhile, in the wider world, Israel's former prime minister Ariel Sharon has died aged 85 after being in a coma for eight years following a stroke.

Opinions of the man are sharply divided. Some view him as a military hero, astute politician and a key architect of the modern state of Israel as we know it. Others consider him a ruthless butcher guilty of wholesale savagery against Palestinians.

One thing's for sure – he will be remembered.

January 14 – It's my great mate Sharon Hirst's birthday today. Happy birthday Shaz, my treasured faith healer. I often wonder where you are and what you're up to these days.

We lost contact several years ago when Shaz, one of the closest friends I've ever had, moved back to her native Yorkshire.

But to return to yesterday's topic of the crazed media obsession with sex.

As if to prove my point, today we were told that a TV soap star was appearing in court accused of raping a 15-year-old girl and a legendary radio DJ was facing charges of sexual assaults on women.

If they're convicted, an outline of the facts should obviously be reported and known. But we certainly don't need blanket coverage of all the sordid details. Not when there's a lot more happening in the world, some of it affecting millions.

Meanwhile, across the Channel, French President Francois Hollande has been accused of having an affair with a film actress.

Mr Hollande didn't deny the allegation, made in a magazine article - but did protest at the invasion of his privacy.

His partner Valerie Trierweiler remains in hospital after having been admitted on Friday. Her aides told French media that she had suffered "shock" after seeing the revelations.

BBC News showed French citizens being interviewed in the street. One young feller said the affair allegation did not alter his opinions of the man as a politician. Thank you!

I've been saying for quite a while that people's private lives should be kept separate from their public achievements. The French and other neighbour communities seem bemused by the English compulsion to confuse the two.

A top politician, sporting, pop or movie star might be a thoroughly nasty person. But that doesn't detract from their brilliance in their chosen field.

We may not like them, but we should be adult enough to appreciate their skills.

Elsewhere in the news, more than 200 South Sudan refugees have drowned in a Nile ferry accident while fleeing fighting in the town of Malakal, the BBC told us today.

Changing the subject completely, I had a thought yesterday evening while watching TV (yes, it happens quite a lot).

It's often said that a brave person is fearless. But when you think about it, this is nonsense. In fact, being fearless – having no fear – makes it impossible to be brave.

Real courage comes when someone's scared witless but faces grave danger anyway.

And, while we're on the subject of popular words and phrases, I've long been hearing the one about necessity being the mother of invention. But there's a new cliché on the block – assumption is the mother of all screw-ups.

That may well be true, but when you think about it, much of our lives are based on assumptions by necessity. You know, that famous mother on invention.

People assume they can trust others, particularly those in authority. They assume that politicians, priests, doctors and media folk are telling them the truth.

They assume that bosses will pay them for work, that the state will help them if they hit on hard times, that the food they eat and water they drink is alright, that friends won't betray or steal from them, and that the justice system will protect them.

Also, we're forced so often to use assumption in order to fill in the gaps when someone's being deliberately cryptic, vague, non-committal or evasive – which can happen quite a lot.

Far too many folk – especially in the media - also seem to assume that government statements and statistics and the bold assertions of Cameron and Osborne are true.

I've often made known my deep resentment for the words and actions of these dreadful men. I don't trust them at all. But do I hate them? – are they my enemies?

On the surface, the answer seems to be a resounding yes. But at a deeper level, they aren't my enemies at all, or anyone else's. We're all parts of the same Oneness.

But they, and certain others, choose to make themselves enemies of others by their atrocious words and deeds.

We should hate the behaviour but not the people. The huge problem with this altruistic ideal is that some folk seem to go out of their way to make us detest them.

As you ponder all that, I shall leave you with my thought for the day - death doesn't come when your heart stops, but when you lose hope.

January 15 – I always get a bit suspicious when defendants are brought to court charged with offences said to date back decades. This has happened again with two celebrities in the news this week.

I ask the question – why, oh why, didn't the apparent victims not report the alleged crimes at the time they were said to have been committed?

Maybe they did, but weren't believed, or possibly the police had insufficient hard evidence. And if they didn't come forward, there could be a variety of reasons.

New facts might have come to light in the interim years, making prosecution possible. Victims may have been too young, naïve, unsure or frightened when the crimes occurred. Or they might have been blackmailed, emotionally or otherwise.

But, if they did keep quiet at the time, only to first mention it eventually to the police many years afterwards, I can't help wondering why.

The cynic in me detects malicious intent, and in the case of claims against the rich and famous, a spot of glory hunting, gold digging or mischief-making.

If they had originally feared reprisals and felt intimidated and threatened, as some may well claim, surely those threats would still be there.

Age and dateline don't matter - if you've upset the wrong people they can still send someone to find and kill or harm you – or at least scare you into silence.

Assuming they're still alive, that is. And if not, what on Earth is the point of bringing charges years later anyway? They're gone, beyond the law – and all that will do is harm innocent people like their families and friends (assuming they weren't in on it).

Alleged victims would be forced to re-live ordeals, more people would suffer and no-one would benefit. Justice still wouldn't be served – you can't punish a corpse.

You can, however, tarnish a dead person's name forever – by holding a public inquiry. Lessons can be learnt and hopefully acted upon in a bid to prevent further offences being committed.

And if all parties are still with us, surely they've all led lives for decades since, growing older and, hopefully, wiser. Apart from the more serious cases, the past should be left in the past, or the matter dealt with away from the criminal courts.

But, to avoid you thinking I disbelieve all retrospective allegations and I'm soft on crime, I do fully accept that there's a 50-50 chance the complainant is actually telling the truth. If so, the offender should be punished on a scale matching the offence.

I also agree that a genuine victim could be speaking out years later because they're older and braver, no longer caring what danger they might be putting themselves in.

And when I say serious cases, I mean war crimes, murder, and the more extreme incidents of personal assaults involving violence, maiming with weapons, callous exploitation, brutal control and treatment or physical, sexual or mental anguish.

Allegations of major fraud, robbery and deception might also be brought to court up to years afterwards – provided there's sufficient evidence to secure a conviction.

But certainly not relatively trivial matters such as some of those that are now being highlighted simply because the alleged offenders are well-known. I'm not saying let people get away with wrongdoing - just asking we put things in perspective. We've all done bad stuff so don't be too judgemental of others and don't take up police and criminal court time with retrospective minor matters that could be dealt with in other ways, such as through the civil courts or public inquiries.

Don't get hung up on a past you can't alter. He who is without sin and all that.

Some of the claims of sexual assault and harassment we're now being told about involve very famous TV and radio stars – childhood heroes, household names.

While I remain deeply sceptical about the time delays, I do agree that the scale of the complaints and number of plaintiffs might suggest there's no smoke without fire and there's been serious widespread intimidation and cover-ups over the years. If so, that's disgraceful and the perpetrators most certainly should be reprimanded.

I still say, however, that this mad compulsion to prosecute decades after alleged crimes are said to have occurred is further proof of a very sad fact – some people are so held back by the past they're unable to live in the present.

I prefer to take the view that, apart from extreme cases like those mentioned above, mistakes, aberrations and hurt from earlier times should be left there. Let them go, move on and concentrate on the now with all its joy and challenges.

Don't beat yourself up over things you can't change. Instead, alter the things you can for the better, dwell in the present and look to the future.

Remember the good times by all means, but don't live in the past – for that can be highly destructive. Look at all the unnecessary bloodshed and misery caused by wars centred on old grievances, conflicts and casualties.

Draw a line under them and build a future based on forgiveness, mutual respect, harmony and peace.

January 16 – There's been sad news in the world of comedy – Roger Lloyd-Pack has passed on, aged 69.

His most famous role was as dopey Trigger, Del Boy's lifelong friend in Only Fools and Horses. He played it brilliantly, as deadpan as you can get.

He was also Owen, the lewd and crude farmer in the Vicar of Dibley, and played a variety of other comic and straight acting roles over the years. He made millions laugh and will be sorely missed.

The rest of today's news was the usual mix of the shocking, worrying and interesting.

It included stories about a missing boy, celebrities accused of bribery and sex offences, an alleged paedophile ring using live internet links, concern over defence budget cuts, football results and transfers, and a breakthrough in tackling blindness.

****

CHAPTER SEVEN – PREFERENCES

January 19 – The missing boy has been found – dead. Three-year-old Mikaeel Kular's body was discovered in woodland at Fife, Scotland. His mother has been arrested and charged in connection with the incident. How shocking and tragic.

Switching to lighter matters, I've often mentioned my favourite tunes, albums, musicians and song composers. Now it's the turn of TV, films, actors and writers.

Telly I like watching includes Family Guy, American Dad, Russell Howard's Good News, Only Fools and Horses, Father Ted, Dad's Army, Monty Python, Two Pints, Ideal, Little Britain, Birds of a Feather, Mongrels, the Inbetweeners, Fawlty Towers, Miranda, Nighty Night, Shameless, Fresh Meat, Coming of Age, the Comic Strip, the Vicar of Dibley, the Good Life, One Foot in the Grave, Green Wing, Sherlock, New Tricks, Inspector Morse, Hamish Macbeth, Midsomer Murders (Nettles era), Hustle, Waking the Dead, Silent Witness, Inspector George Gently, Jonathan Creek, Red Dwarf, Kung Fu, Life on Mars, Emmerdale, Coronation Street and EastEnders.

Movies: Fantasia, Close Encounters, Poltergeist, Stargate, the Wicker Man (original), the Exorcist, the Omen series, the Hammer horrors, the Matrix and Terminator films, the Hobbit/Lord of the Rings movies, Kill Bill One and Two, Lock, Stock and Two Smoking Barrels, Psycho, Snatch, Love, Honour and Obey, Green Street, the Football Factory,

Twin Town, the Boat that Rocked, Eat the Rich, Human Traffic, the Da Vinci Code, Highlander, Help, a Hard Day's Night, Yellow Submarine, the Python films, the Carry Ons, Mel Brooks' movies, Airplane One and Two, Trainspotting, Love Actually, Titanic, Four Weddings and a Funeral and Coyote Ugly.

Favourite actors include John Hurt, Spencer Tracy, Glenda Jackson, Alec Guinness, Tom Hanks, John Gielgud, Ralph Richardson, Oliver Reed, Liza Minnelli, Richard Harris, Peter O'Toole, Elizabeth Taylor, Bette Davis, Henry, Jane and Peter Fonda, Steve McQueen, Sean Connery, Jodi Foster, Colin Firth, Jason Statham, John Wayne, Bob Hope, Dustin Hoffman, Johnny Depp, Robert Redford, Jack Lemmon, Ewan McGregor, Anne Bancroft, Paul Newman, John Thaw, David Jason, Pauline Quirke, Joanna Lumley, Helen Mirren, Robert Carlyle, Bob Hoskins and Leonard Rossiter.

My favourite writers include William Shakespeare, Charles Dickens, Jane Austen, George Bernard Shaw, Lewis Carroll, Dylan Thomas, William Blake, Percy and Mary Shelley, Lord Byron, John Keats, Edgar Allan Poe, Bram Stoker, Samuel Taylor Coleridge, Dennis Wheatley, Jack Kerouac, Martina Cole, Mark Twain, Arthur Conan Doyle, Jean-Paul Sartre, J R R Tolkien, Michael Moorcock, Anthony Burgess, Robert Pirsig, Douglas Adams, Simon Schama, David Icke and Dan Brown.

Scriptwriters: John Sullivan, Richard Curtis, Dick Clement and Ian La Frenais, David Croft, Jimmy Perry, Jeremy Lloyd, Rob Grant and Doug Naylor, Laurence Marks and Maurice Gran, Roy Clarke, Rowan Atkinson, David Renwick, Johnny Speight, Spike Milligan, David Nobbs, Simon Nye, Roy Mitchell and the other New Tricks writers, the Sherlock, Inspector Morse, Doctor Who, Monty Python, Fawlty

Towers, Not the Nine O'clock News and Drop the Dead Donkey teams.

While I'm in the mood for listing things, I shall return to music briefly to give a run down of my 50 favourite albums:

1, Dark Side of the Moon – Pink Floyd; 2, Revolver – the Beatles; 3, Sergeant Pepper – the Beatles; 4, Wish You Were Here – Pink Floyd; 5, Abbey Road – the Beatles; 6, Rubber Soul – the Beatles; 7, White Album – the Beatles; 8, A Hard Day's Night – the Beatles; 9, The Wall – Pink Floyd; 10, Led Zeppelin Two – Led Zeppelin, 11, Close to the Edge – Yes; 12 – Who's Next – the Who; 13, John Lennon Plastic Ono Band – John Lennon; 14, Selling England by the Pound – Genesis; 15, Aqualung – Jethro Tull; 16, Marquee Moon – Television; 17, Sticky Fingers – the Rolling Stones; 18, All Things Must Pass – George Harrison, 19, Heaven and Hell – Black Sabbath; 20, Quadrophenia – the Who;

21, Tubular Bells – Mike Oldfield; 22, Led Zeppelin Four - Led Zeppelin; 23, Catch a Fire – the Wailers; 24, In Rock – Deep Purple; 25, Ziggy Stardust – David Bowie ; 26, Tommy – the Who; 27, Pet Sounds – the Beach Boys; 28, Paranoid –Black Sabbath; 29, Let it Be – the Beatles; 30, Pilgrimage – Wishbone Ash; 31, Goodbye Yellow Brick Road – Elton John; 32, Definitely Maybe – Oasis; 33, Please Please Me-the Beatles; 34, London Calling – the Clash; 35, Band on the Run – Wings; 36, Machine Head - Deep Purple; 37, Velvet Underground and Nico – the Velvet Underground; 38, Never Mind the Bollocks – the Sex Pistols; 39, The River - Bruce Springsteen; 40, Exodus – Bob Marley; 41, Disintegration – the Cure; 42, The Joshua Tree – U2, 43, Life's Rich Pageant – REM; 44, Back in Black – AC/DC; 45, Nevermind -Nirvana; 46, Signing Off –UB40; 47, Twenty-five Years On - Hawklords; 48, Easter – Patti Smith; 49, the Hounds of Love – Kate Bush; 50, Appetite for Destruction – Guns'n'Roses.

Several brilliant artists released terrific singles but their albums were patchy, such as Elvis Presley, Bob Dylan, the Bee Gees, Abba, Rod Stewart, the Faces/Small Faces, Slade, Motorhead, the Pogues, the Shadows, Alice Cooper, Eminem, Blur and Frankie Goes to Hollywood.

The Beatles (together and solo), the Rolling Stones, Jimi Hendrix, Tom Petty, Simon and Garfunkel, the Who, the Jam, Oasis, Fleetwood Mac, Hawkwind, the Police, REM, Queen, the Jam and David Bowie also produced a lot of fantastic songs but some of their long-players were similarly a bit hit-and-miss.

Best bands – 1, the Beatles; 2, Led Zeppelin; 3, Pink Floyd; 4, the Who; 5, the Rolling Stones; 6, Genesis; 7, Yes; 8, Fleetwood Mac; 9, Hawkwind/Hawklords; 10, Black Sabbath; 11, the Doors: 12, Deep Purple; 13, AC/DC; 14, the Shadows, 15, U2; 16, Oasis; 17, Cream; 18,the Beach Boys; 19, the Clash; 20, Iron Maiden; 21, the Smiths; 22, Queen; 23, the Sex Pistols; 24, REM; 25, Blur; 26, Emerson, Lake and Palmer; 27, the Jam; 28, UB40; 29, Motorhead; 30, Wishbone Ash.

Solo male – 1, John Lennon; 2, Jimi Hendrix; 3, Paul McCartney; 4, Bob Marley; 5, George Harrison; 6, David Bowie; 7, Elton John; 8, Elvis Presley; 9, Bruce Springsteen; 10, Buddy Holly; 11, Chuck Berry; 12, Roy Orbison; 13, Eric Clapton, 14, Johnny Cash, 15, Tom Petty, 16, Ozzy Osbourne; 17, Eminem; 18, Rory Gallagher; 19, Alice Cooper; 20, Gary Moore.

Female – 1, Kate Bush; 2, Joni Mitchell; 3, Janis Joplin; 4, Dusty Springfield; 5, Stevie Nicks; 6, Patti Smith; 7, Madonna; 8, Aretha Franklin; 9, Tina Turner; 10, Amy Winehouse; 11, Adele; 12, Elkie Brooks; 13, Kylie Minogue; 14, Lulu; 15, Kate Nash; 16, Pink; 17, Lily Allen; 18, Sinead O'Connor; 19, Annie Lennox; 20, Cilla Black.

Like I said, I like writing lists.

But, you might ask, what about Pearl Jam, the Cure, Madness, Status Quo, Simple Minds, Rainbow, the Kinks, Judas Priest, UFO, the Hollies, the Police, Guns N' Roses, Nirvana, Wings, Echo and the Bunnymen, Thin Lizzy, Free, Gillan, King Crimson, the Faces, Lynyrd Skynyrd, Eddie and the Hot Rods, the Undertones, Metallica, Joy Division, the Pet Shop |Boys and the Electric Light Orchestra?

It's a fair point, and I do love all these bands too. The live sets I saw by Quo, Gillan, the Kinks, Thin Lizzy, UFO and the Undertones were among the best I've ever seen. They're all excellent groups, but did not quite make my all-time top 30.

Similarly, you could cite Bridge Over Troubled Water, What's the Story, the Snow Goose, In Search of Space, Hunky Dory, Screamadelica, New Boots and Panties, Days of the Future Passed, Exile on Main Street, Parallel Lines, Moving Waves, Houses of the Holy, a Night at the Opera, Levitation, Combat Rock, Horses, Harvest, Master of Puppets, A Trick of the Tail, Darkness of the Edge of Town, Rumours, the Sensual World, What's Going On? , Electric Ladyland, the Icicle Works, Animals, Help!, the Queen is Dead, Love Over Gold, Making Movies, Let it Bleed, Argus, Wind and Wuthering, Script for a Jester's Tear, Bridge of Sighs and War as great albums –and I would wholeheartedly agree.

But these are bloody tough categories for me because I love rock and pop music so much in all its glorious forms. I guess what I'm trying to do is give you an overall view of my wide tastes in all these fields.

If I had to pick 50 albums, a limited list of TV programmes or movies, or certain writers' work to keep me entertained depending on what mood I'm in, these would pretty much be them.

I do, however, draw the line at even attempting to pick my top 20, 30, or even 200 songs – there are so many fantastic tunes out there that it's an impossible task.

As always happens, others will challenge my choices and the order I've placed them in. It could be a topic for hot debate. But it's my book and my lists as I sit here typing my preferences on to this computer screen today.

I could change my mind tomorrow, or next week, month or year. I could well alter the orders of some entries, dropping certain ones and replacing them with others. We're all allowed revisions and rethinks, aren't we?

Having referred to many of these people, books, programmes, films and musical collections in passing in previous volumes, I thought it was high time I wrote down some more comprehensive summaries of my tastes. Just so you know.

If you're still reading, that is, and not chosen to skip the last few pages. If you have, fair enough. Welcome back.

January 20 – Weird, innit? We seem to spend so much time arguing about who's done what to whom when it's vociferously denied, totally overlooking the need to reprimand those who not only admit their crimes but are actually proud of them.

Terrorists boldly claim responsibility for their actions in order to make political points – and in their case, yes of course they should be punished but at the same time we should be asking important questions as to why they did what they did.

That way, we can attempt to solve problems by removing the grievances that cause hostility and friction, and hopefully then progress towards a more peaceful future.

I was actually thinking more of government leaders who pick on and penalise their own citizens. They should be ousted at the next election and then dealt with severely, maybe even imprisoned for their recklessness and neglect – depending on the scale of their policies' impact.

For, let's face it, they've made no bones about their actions – freely admitting them and even boasting about them. They've been callous, spiteful and unfair – all very serious offences in my opinion.

Okay, I accept that I sometimes come out with controversial opinions, but they're usually said with tongue lodged firmly in cheek. I feel it's a humorous and colourful way of hammering home my serious points.

And I'm not the only one prone to making outrageous, quite extreme statements – people do it on Facebook and in conversation all the time. Even nice, kind, decent, mild-mannered folk.

Similarly driven by deep concern and frustration, they're also doing it to create the maximum impact – well, I hope so, anyway, because if I thought for one moment they were serious I'd start to get very worried!

But back to our pesky government - while incredibly suspicious of the motives behind its actions, I do actually support some of its policy decisions. Credit where it's due, and all that.

The latest is the new ruling that people should be able to speak and read English in order to receive state benefits, announced on this morning's TV news.

I happen to believe that people living in our country should be able to use its native tongue – just like English folk living abroad should learn their new country's language without question.

Some would consider this a racist statement, but I passionately disagree. To think that is to confuse ignorant and abhorrent xenophobia with practical common sense – just like moves to control the numbers of people flocking to our shores.

How on Earth can anyone get by without being able to communicate in their host country's language? Okay, speaking to others from their own land in their own tongue is fine - normal in fact - but it beggars belief that some think they can avoid being able to communicate with any country's wider population.

I mean, to state the obvious, how the hell could they read the forms they'd need to fill in to claim benefit anyway? Or any other versions of the written word, for that matter – pamphlets, newspapers, signs, posters, labels, instructions, books and so on?

I would have thought it was a basic requirement for anyone living in a land other than their own birthplace.

Having said all that, common sense or not, I still deeply suspect the real reasons behind this new policy. I see another cynical attempt to bash foreigners and benefit claimants while saving cash on the welfare bill.

In other words, another bid to protect and pander to the politicians' own sinister little clique by hassling and penalising the wider population – the common herd.

January 22 – Happy birthday John – Gaynor, that is. Have a fab one mate!

I like incense sticks. I have various types of Nag Champa plus Kashmir Sandal and Maharani Heena. Burning them in rotation leaves your living room smelling of a gorgeous mixture of them all. Nice!

January 23 – In my last book, Scratched Crystal, I referred to ridiculously persistent mates – the ones who won't take no for an answer. Now I shall turn to the I'm perfect, I'm always right and I know best brigades.

Often these are the same annoying people, but not always.

We all like to impose our wills on situations, assert our authority, state our case and get our own way. It's a natural, perfectly normal human response to situations and events.

But some do it to an irritating degree, so wrapped up are they in what they want that they're totally regardless of others' views or feelings. They're a pain in the bum.

Take the I'm perfect crowd for example. These folk constantly criticise others but refuse to accept their own flaws and limitations.

The I'm always right merchants have an opinion on all matters and are convinced it's a valid one - whether or not they have any knowledge of the subject under discussion.

But sometimes the I know best crew are the most infuriating of all. We've all met them - they always know better than you what you should do in any given situation, arrogantly attempting to persuade you they're right and you're wrong.

You feel like screaming at these people - "piss off – it's my life and my decision" or "you're wrong you know" or "shut the hell up until you know what you're talking about."

Friends are always asking me what I think about this or that. When I reply – "I don't know really, haven't given it much thought" they will start to press me for an opinion on something I know little or nothing about. How mad is that?

For, to state the obvious, my view is bound to be at least a bit suspect if I'm unfamiliar with the facts.

Okay, we can all express opinions about things we know little or nothing about. Often it's done in a bid to release anger, frustration or pent-up concern when our hearts tell us something's very wrong – evil, immoral or unfair.

Again, this is a perfectly natural, normal human response. But some of us have the grace to accept we're mistaken or misguided if facts are presented to us challenging our views and comments.

Speaking personally, if I'm not sure I'm right, I'll always give way to someone who seems to know more about the topic under discussion.

But if I know damned well I'm right, I'll stick to my guns. I can be stubborn like that. In those cases I ask if we can agree to differ, to avoid any further friction or argument.

And, talking of arguments, I read something the other day that is so true. Extending the olive branch and apologising after a row doesn't necessarily mean you're accepting you were wrong – but it does show you're a decent person for not letting a silly disagreement cause lasting damage.

****

CHAPTER EIGHT – CELEBRATIONS

January 26 – Chuffed ain't the word! A few days ago I received my paperback copies of Sunshine and Ice Volumes Three to Six, prior to their publication over the next few weeks. They'll go online via Kindle/Amazon in due course.

So most of my written works will be out there, so to speak, with only this volume remaining unpublished. I'll complete it soon and send it to Indepenpress for printing and release under the same terms as the others. Then I'll start volume eight.

I've received good feedback from friends and family who have read the first two volumes, and I've now started handing out the just-received Volumes 3-6 paperbacks to mates. I'll give Phil and Emily, Carol and David and Suzette their copies when I next see them.

Others will be posted or given out to friends in the coming days and weeks.

I gave Sam and Carl their copies when I saw them on Friday (today being a Sunday). I also popped copies of volumes 3-6 round Kerry's for her and Theresa.

Sam invited me back to theirs yesterday, too, and all in all it was a very good weekend with them, Rudy, Bailey, Becca, Tina, Sharon, Jem and Jimmy.

Becca has a new puppy, an early present for her birthday in May. He's a very cute little terrier-Shih Tzu cross and she's decided to call him Albert.

January 28 – This morning's TV news announced that the economy is growing again and unemployment is at its lowest level for years. Oh really? Please excuse my scepticism but I don't believe a word of it.

How the hell can either statement be true when the country's still reeling from the savage cutbacks and wholesale job losses resulting from the coalition's drive to destroy and decimate?

I don't trust any so-called facts and figures put out by this God-awful regime. I suspect massive distortion of the picture to make it appear like our callous overlords' dreadful policies are working.

Even if the statements are true – very unlikely, in my humble opinion – I would ask at what cost in human suffering? What's the point of any economic recovery if people are sick, dying, poverty-stricken and miserable as a consequence of iron fist governmental decisions?

In other words, what price compassion, humanity and decency?

The coalition carve-up merchants say more deep cuts are on the way because they still haven't managed to fully remedy Labour's disastrous mishandling of our economy. This excuse gets flimsier by the month. How long do they need to put things right?

My scepticism over this whole "the country's skint" allegation is well documented. But even if times are hard and belt-tightening is needed, this lot are going about it completely the wrong way by hitting vulnerable people hard instead of saving billions on costly material stuff.

I accept that some savings might be – and I stress might be – needed. For example, that troublesome ash cloud back in 2010 didn't help and no doubt caused some lasting damage. But is the situation as serious as the government claims? I think not.

They're playing their favourite game of divide and rule while blaming the previous Labour administration for everything.

But you can't pin the ash cloud crisis on Brown and Co for starters, which is probably why that's not mentioned much these days. External factors might also come into play to a certain extent – but surely an important part of the government's job is to shield and protect us from these!

February 3 – The country faces a stark choice when it comes to flood defence, the Environment Agency announced today. Should we protect urban or rural areas?

Both, you idiots! Ah, but, they say, we don't have a bottomless purse and can't afford it all so we must choose.

Says who? As I've just asked in a different context, isn't protecting citizens one of the government's main jobs, no matter where they live?

This is yet another classic divide and rule tactic – setting sections of society railing against each other in a cruel and cynical way. I find that disgusting.

And it will really rankle with the anxious victims of recent flooding as the weather turned unusually violent and destructive. They're already fuming at the government's slow and inadequate response to the crisis.

A 73-year-old male cyclist died and thousands have suffered massively from the damage caused to homes, farmland and so on.

But as flood-hit communities enjoy a brief respite from the bad weather, forecasters are warning worse could be on the way. Charming!

February 4 – Excellent news on the pub front – yes, it is going to be called The Bell again! Mark and Laura have passed their probationary period and are now the official new managers.

They said just after taking over that they wanted to revert to the old name if the brewery accepted them on a five-year lease – and now it looks like both are happening.

Like many of the old crowd who are drifting back now, I thought Seabourne's was a daft name. It's always been the Bell to us, and always will be. Welcome back, friend, we've missed you!

February 6 – A crown court jury this morning cleared Coronation Street actor Bill Roache of two rapes and four indecent assaults.

Mr Roache, 81, is apparently the world's longest-serving soap star, having been in the programme since its very first episode in December 1960. He's not appeared in it since being charged last May, but today it was strongly hinted he may return soon.

Five women had claimed he assaulted them years ago when they were teenagers.

I told in Scratched Crystal how I met him once. A local newspaper reporter at the time, I was sent with a photographer to cover his opening of a new supermarket in New Milton. It was a very brief encounter, but he seemed an okay guy.

His acquittal today shows just how careful we must be about slinging mud at others. Some is bound to stick even if, as in his case, they are subsequently vindicated.

Our gutter press should learn a lesson from this. But they won't because they specialise in sensational claims pillorying celebrities in the total absence of any court-tested hard facts. Reputations are ruined but they don't care – It sells newspapers.

Such careless and callous witch-hunts deflect attention from real cases of violent abuse and brutal exploitation. The innocent are demonised while the guilty escape prosecution. And I find that abhorrent.

Meanwhile, Nick Clegg (boo, hiss!) has once again shown what an unreliable turncoat he really is.

Making a party political broadcast for the Lib Dems, shown on TV last night, he asserted that it was in Britain's interest to stay in Europe and play a key role – and he warned that it would be disastrous to try and extricate ourselves, as UKIP want.

Not all that long ago – before he tasted power – I welcomed his warning against too much involvement in Europe and his resistance to calls from both Labour and the Tories for further integration. Politicians, eh? - What a trustworthy bunch!

February 11 – Thousands of people have been seriously hit by the worst UK flooding since records began. Citizens in Somerset, Berkshire, Surrey and Worcestershire are incensed at the government's slow response as rivers have deluged homes and farms.

Meanwhile, in America, Former Hollywood child star Shirley Temple has died at the age of 85.

The actress found fame as a young girl in the 1930s in films like Bright Eyes, Stand Up and Cheer and Curly Top.

After retiring from films in 1950 at the age of 21, she returned to the public eye as a Republican candidate for Congress and as a US diplomat. She died on Monday at home in Woodside, California, from natural causes.

February 14 – Happy Valentine's Day folks. And many congats to Rachel, Emily's sister, who gave birth to a baby girl, Lily Rose, yesterday.

In the wider world, the rain continues to bucket down as more gale-force winds batter our fair land. Coastal areas are being deluged by the sea as more inland rivers burst their banks, flooding homes and property causing untold damage.

****

The year 2014 is a landmark one in several respects. We've just passed the 50th anniversary of the Beatles' arrival in America on February 9, 1964 – a pivotal moment in music history.

I'm poised to celebrate my 60th birthday. And several people I know are 50 this year, including my ex-wife Joe and her twin sister Cheryl and my mates Jem, Carl and Russell.

So now seems a perfect time to review my life. I'm delighted to have made it this far – especially in light of my heart issues – and, whatever happens now, I've enjoyed an existence packed with fun times and I have a glittering array of fond memories.

Sure, I've had years of drudgery, hassle, tragedy and heartache. But I count myself extremely lucky to have also had the constant love and support of family and friends.

We've had some fantastic shared experiences. I've mentioned many of them in my books.

So, as I reach my diamond anniversary, I look back with a lot of affection on great times with great people. And I feel that, at long last, I've realised my dream – with six volumes of my journal either published or about to be and this one nearing its completion.

I'm going to finish it now and send it off to my publishers for release in paperback and on Kindle/Amazon under the same terms as the rest.

As for the future, who knows? How long I've got left and how things will pan out are mysteries to be revealed as time unfolds. One thing's for sure – I'm on the last lap now and the finishing line will soon be coming into view.

That's not being morbid, just realistic. It's great to still be here – especially when family members and mates have already passed over - and I view each day as a blessing. I'll just poodle along, hopefully smiling, until it's my time to go too.

February 19 – Its tea-time and I've just been watching my favourite TV quiz show, The Chase. Smiling participants introduce themselves thus: "Hello, I'm Bert; I'm 54 and a truck driver from Cleethorpes."

As if ages and occupations are that frigging important. Hello, I'm Martin, 59, and a bum from Bournemouth. Daft, innit?

Earlier on, I watched the Jeremy Kyle Show and, as usual, that awful, opinionated talk show host was berating a young guy because he didn't have a job. Okay, this feller was objectionable, but he would have been that anyway, work or no work.

Kyle said if he had his way, he'd stop all welfare payments to people who sat on their bums all day and spent their benefit money on booze and weed.

Why? If claimants stupidly use vital lifeline cash to buy lager and drugs instead of food, provisions and shelter, surely that's they're look out and none of his business – Unless they're addicts or have mental problems, in which case they should be offered help in coping with their issues and managing their limited funds.

And if they do blow all their benefits on cans and booze, at least they will be paying tax on those cans, therefore putting something back into the system! The same would apply to baccy or fags.

It wouldn't apply to the weed, of course – but could do if it was legalised and made taxable.

Okay, those last two comments were a bit facetious but I hope you get the point. We all pay money to the government on everything we buy whether we're working or not – expecting and trusting our leaders to spend it benefiting us all in various ways.

But these coalition cut-throats have dashed those expectations and betrayed that trust with their savage policies hitting the poor, elderly and disabled hardest.

Like I've said before, I do find that Kyle programme interesting viewing but its horrible host gives me the right hump!

February 24 – I've already stated that, when it comes to crime, we all have our own pet hates and we can all be outrageous hypocrites, blasting certain types of wrongdoer while ignoring, passively accepting or even condoning the behaviour of others.

My own bugbear is violent crime – the very worst kind in my opinion. I feel those that savagely assault others should be dealt with the harshest. Crimes against kids also rankle.

But brutal mental abuse is despicable, disgusting and diabolical. Twisting perceptions, brainwashing and the clinical use of mind control, with or without the aid of drugs, is both very wrong and positively terrifying.

Yet both are sanctioned by the military, and justified by the comment that other nations employ physical and mental abuse so we have to in order to effectively combat such tactics. I can't argue, but I still say it's abhorrent – a sad comment on the messed-up state of our world.

And, when addressing any type of hurtful action, or any kind of crime for that matter, we always need to take into account a variety of factors including the circumstances, context, severity, extent of damage done, mitigating circumstances, possible justifications and the perpetrator's state of mind.

February 25 – Well, today's the day – I've made it to the Big Six-O. So how do I feel? Not much different, as it goes. Another day, another year.

This morning's been bright and sunny and I took a shower to help energize me for the celebrations. Yesterday, I had a haircut. So I'm feeling all spruced, shiny and new.

I opened my cards and lit a candle in memory of George Harrison, born February 25, 1943, died November 29, 2001. I also put a tribute to him on Facebook, where some mates had posted happy birthday messages to me – bless 'em.

Carol and David had put some money in a brilliant home-made 60th birthday card. It's weird – even at the age of 60, I'm still the baby of the family and always will be.

February 25, five hours later – I've just got back from a lovely Toby Carvery lunch with Suzette – her treat for my landmark anniversary. She also gave me cookies, Mars Bars and a W H Smiths gift card – terrific!

We toasted the occasion and remembered our beloved Jan, who would have been with us had she still been alive. Carol and David couldn't join us this time as they had other commitments.

Other cards have arrived, some with money in, and more friends have posted nice messages on Facebook.

My birthday present to myself is a CD of Ellie Goulding's superb album Halcyon Days. This highly talented singer-songwriter, multi-instrumentalist and actress is a festival favourite and one of the brightest new stars in the rock firmament.

So I now stride out in the sunshine to a new decade of my life in this reality, relieved that I've made it this far and wondering how long I've still got and what the future holds for me, my loved ones and the planet.

Whatever happens for now on, I've had some great times with family and friends amid all the misery and madness, drudgery and dread. And for that I thank the Universe with all my heart.

So that's about it – at least for now. Apart from tidying up a few loose ends, that is…

****

CHAPTER NINE – CONCLUSION

So I guess it's time to draw this section of my junk-cluttered journal to a close. I shall leave you with the following thought:

We're all mad in various degrees and we live in an insane world run by ruthless, unscrupulous crazies. The good news is that for every dangerous nutter, there are at least five harmless head cases to cheer us up. Thank goodness for likeable loons!

Seize the carp.

Love and peace, Martin Money, February 25, 2014.

****

Now for the PS bit, comprising mentions for those who have featured in my life…

First and foremost, Phil, Emily, Chloe, Lucas and Harvey, Carol, David, Suzette, Joyce, and all the rellies, here and passed on.

Three special women – Joe, Dawn and Paula.

Cheryl, Mark, Ben, Kayleigh, Aaron, Rachel, Lily, Simon, Gail, Keith, Ali, Terry, Roxanna, Stuart and Brian – in fact, the combined clans of the Moneys, Dixons, Coopers, Quilters, Hurleys, Collins', Painters and all associated with them.

Sam, Carl and family; Carole, Tom, Chris and their daughters; Linda W, Steve Y and his kids, Jill, Lesley, John Pants, Stuart, Steve, Jem, Tony, Fiona, Bridget, Martine and the rest of the Hannen brood; Rich and Sam, Rod, Andy, Roz, Helen, Gadget, Jeff and Tina, Chris and Lou, Darren and Tara, Skinny, Nathan and Ping.

Shaz, Lea, Steve T, John H, Torben, The Dominoes, Sue, Lorna, June, Noreen, Patsy, Lisa, Lyn and the Krypton/Mace crew.

Kerry, Claire, Theresa, Ryan, Steve E, Sean, Mick and Baby-face Pete.

John G, John P, Matt and Dani, Ben, Jenny, Quizmaster Steve, Chappie, Vicky and Mark, Lee, Squeak, Scott, Jim, Billy, the two Kellys, Maria H, Ollie O, Chelsea Nige, Tamsin, Sam, Becky and other bar staff, Mark, Callum and Laura and all at The Bell.

Brian and Jan, Phil and Jane, Julie, Big Sam, Tina, Maria S, Paul and Sarah, Debs and Alan, Bev, Michelle, Mick and Ro, Dave Spoon, Bill, Birdseye, Irish Pat, Irish Paul, Sean and Kevin H, Chelsea Pete, Sharon, Carol, Scottish Dave, Man U Martin, Chelsea Bob, Celtic Nicky and Gary the Sheep.

Andy, Jerry, Steve G and all the Home Guard reprobates; the Pinecliff posse.

Jen C, Tara S, Emily, Brun, Lisa; Trudy, Lou and family; Julia, Geordie Ken, Crystal, Aussie Stu, Ray and Monica, Flavie, Ian, Saskia and Linda F.

Jaymi, Clare H, Candice, Deano, Dottie, Jane M, Tich, Lucy, Craig, Keenan, Dan S, Nick, Paul S and his dad Mike.

Cass, Sonia, Bricktop Tina, Sharon, Russell, Jac, Jimmy and the Roberts Road randoms. My landlords Barry and Ray.

Milk Marketing Martin, Steve M, Terry S, Chris Z, Chris T, John C, Dave T, Steve B, Terry L, Pete M, Mick and Steve C, Kevin F, Kay, Nick, Eileen, Sue and Chris.

Ann and family, Dave R, Robin T, Alex C, Justin S, Peter E, Laurence D, Mike G and others I've worked with.

Janet U, Pauline S, Karen M, Lynne H, Jill S, Rita L and Janet K; Hawkie Hawkins, the Goodmans, Ray and Hazel, Jerry and Maureen.

Rudy the dog and the cats, Lily and Billy; Kelloggs and Albert.

Lemmy, Biff Byford, Bill Wyman, Jon Anderson, Ernie Wise, Lionel Blair, Pat Phoenix, Tony Booth, Richard Branson, Frank Bough, Russ Abbot, Bill Roache and other famous folk I've spoken to or met.

All my Facebook friends, who have also given me many hours of great entertainment.

If I've forgotten anyone, I apologise. If you've touched my life with friendship, affection, joy and experiences then you're included too.

And just in case you were wondering – yes, I am Jim.

****

Those things I thought were carved in stone were scrawled in shifting sand.

The corridors of power have many dark corners.

Atheists can be angels too, you know.

Do what you can to help the positive vibration disperse the politics of separation. Spread the joy, shine a light, foster peace and harmony – you know it makes sense!

Love is the answer – no matter what the question.

Some people are so poor, all they have is money.

Death doesn't come when your heart stops, but when you lose hope.

****

This book is dedicated, with much affection, to my dear family and brilliant friends who have blessed my life with happiness.

It is written in memory of my mother, father, my son John, sister Jan and all other loved ones who have passed on to the next level.

Also mates who have gone that way, such as Umo, Hairy Pete and Lee.

And treasured family friends – Bill Dutfield, Gladys Weston and Tom Dixon.

The late and legendary Tony Anderson.

It is also presented in honour of the memories and ideals of Nelson Mandela and other champions of peace, harmony and justice no longer in the material world.

"If someone thinks that love and peace is a cliché that must have been left behind in the sixties, that's his problem. Love and peace are eternal."- John Lennon, 9/10/1940 to 8/12/1980.

"We were talking about the space between us all and the people who hide themselves behind a wall of illusion, never glimpse the truth - then it's far too late when they pass away." Lyrics to Within You, Without You by George Harrison, 25/2/1943 to 29/11/2001.

"If we don't do the impossible, we shall be faced with the unthinkable" – German Green activist Petra Kelly, 29/11/1947 to 1/10/1992.

ABOUT THE AUTHOR

Born in Slough on February 25, 1954, Martin Money lived there until early adulthood, moving to Dorset in 1978.

Leaving school with three A levels and seven O levels, he worked in a bank for a few months before starting a 24-year career in regional newspaper journalism that ended in redundancy in 1997.

Since then he's had a variety of part-time jobs and also worked as a volunteer for charities.

A proud father and grandfather, he lives in Bournemouth where he enjoys short cliff top walks, writing, reading, watching TV, listening to music and socialising.

Photo of author by Sam Excell.

www.ingramcontent.com/pod-product-compliance
Lightning Source LLC
Chambersburg PA
CBHW021619270326
41931CB00008B/772

* 9 7 8 1 7 8 0 0 3 7 7 8 3 *